DAPHNE M. MATTHEWS

Published by American Palate
A Division of The History Press
Charleston, SC
www.historypress.com

First published 2020

Manufactured in the United States

ISBN 9781467144711

Library of Congress Control Number: 2020934429

Notice: The information in this book is true and complete to the best of our knowledge. It is offered without guarantee on the part of the author or The History Press. The author and The History Press disclaim all liability in connection with the use of this book.

I would never write a word if not for my mother. She encourages me when I feel I've lost my imagination; she grounds me when my imagination gets too wild. I have been lucky enough to have five extraordinarily strong, independent women in my life. My mother, Patricia Strong Williams; her mother, Edla Haynes Strong; my paternal grandmother, Ruby Rhoton Williams; my great-aunt, Joyce Horton Gill; and a special cousin, Anita Angeletti Shrewsbury, who have all helped me know who I am. I strive to be as strong and independent as they once were. I still feel their strength, even though my mother is the only one still living.

I am also lucky enough to have a great father, Jerry Williams, and sister, Brenda Williams Wallace, who are ever present in my life. My husband, Ronnie, is truly a gift from God, as are our two sons, Joey and Jimmy, and granddaughter, Angel.

I also want to mention three particularly good friends, Angela Valentine Hale, Jenifer Mellons Colorio and Christy Flanary Smith, who encourage me daily, and Lennea Hickam, who came in for a last-minute save for some important information. Last but not least, I would like to thank three aunts who have been a major part of my life since I was born: Lois Williams, Nora Williams Duncan and Juanita "Edie" Williams Adams. These three ladies taught me most of what I know about street smarts.

Unfortunately, death has always been present in my life, and this year has been no different. I would like to dedicate this book to the family and friends who passed on during the writing of this book: Aunts Virginia "Ginny" Hopkins and Mona Williams; uncle-in-law Glen Matthews; cousin-in-law Donnie Baker; family friend Karen Webb; high school classmates and friends Chris Birchfield, Cheyenne Jobe, Heather Scism and John Mark Anderson; longtime friend Michael "Mikey" Mullins; and a cousin who was one of the best friends that I have ever had, Mason Shrewsbury Jr.

To live in hearts we leave behind is not to die.
—Thomas Campbell

Contents

Contents

Preface

I love to write; however, I did not start 2019 with the intention of undertaking such a task as this. In the spring, I queried The History Press about writing a children's history book, but at that time, such a project was not needed. Instead, they suggested I look into authoring a book about restaurants that were beloved by the residents in my area. I was excited. I knew it would be interesting, but I had no idea of the path on which the research would lead me.

I started strong by reaching out to the Kingsport Archives. Brianne Johnson Wright has also written for this publishing house and knew the type of photos I needed. That was a great first start that led to a false sense of security. When my husband and I wrote *Images of America: Hiltons* in 2008, we had a lot of help from the community. We already knew many of those people, but we were authoring a book covering a small physical area of land. However, because of the success of that project, I mistakenly thought this one would be easier to write. Boy, was I wrong.

The main challenge with this book was learning how to reach out to strangers in the social media age. I thought that I would meet with people, they would share photos and stories and I would be able to link the stories together quickly. However, people are so busy that it was hard to meet with former restaurant owners, so I reached out through email, social media and phone calls. I also used online communication for personal touches and published material for the facts. That was the first hurdle. The second was photos. It seems, as I have been told repeatedly in the last few months, that normal people don't take pictures of restaurants. That was a fact I had never considered. People really don't take pictures of restaurants. The vast majority of historic photos included here came from the Kingsport Archives. A few came from smaller groups, and the rest came from my own collection—some of which I took for this very publication.

The third hurdle was that there are way too many restaurants from this area to cover each one. That challenge was decided by availability. I had the most information from Kingsport in Sullivan County. I had some from Hawkins and Washington Counties in Tennessee and Scott County, Virginia. I also had a few that were scattered in Washington County, Virginia, as well as Carter and Greene Counties, Tennessee, but not enough information to do those justice. So, I set these hurdles aside and created a historical collection of some of the best restaurants in our area.

Acknowledgements

There are so many who have helped along the way with this book—too many to mention here, in fact—but I would like to especially thank my husband, Ronnie, and my son Jimmy, who have had to live with me while writing this book. There were days when I was not that easy to live with—or so my family thinks. They were also instrumental in helping me scout locations. What could have been leisurely Sunday afternoon drives became hunts for "that restaurant someone told me was down this way."

I would also like to thank my son Joey and his fiancee, Harley, for their patience. I would like to thank Joey's daughter, Angel, for making me laugh on days I was too stressed to do so otherwise. Grandchildren really are grand.

I want to thank my mom and dad, Pat and Jerry Williams, who made suggestions of restaurants that were before my time. A special thanks to my mother for being a sounding board when I was frustrated.

The Kingsport Archives in the Kingsport Library, particularly Brianne Johnson Wright, was instrumental in collecting photos for the area. I would also like to thank the Scott County Archives, the Heritage Alliance in Jonesborough and the Sullivan County Archives in Blountville. Restaurant owners, past and present, have been an immense help, and former employees of these restaurants were also able to add some color to the stories. The Washington County Public Library in Jonesborough, the Sullivan County Public Library in Blountville and the Kingsport Public Library were all a huge help in finding the pertinent information for this collection. I don't want to leave out the patrons of these establishments because they have given me information and stories that brought these relics to life for me.

I would like to thank Jimmy Neil Smith for contributing the section on the Parson's Table and Widow Brown's, two of the restaurants he has owned through the years.

JIMMY NEIL SMITH

Jimmy Neil Smith graduated from East Tennessee State University in 1969. During high school and college, he wrote for local newspapers. He especially enjoyed his column Heritage in Buckskin, featuring regional history that was published in the *Johnson City Press*. Those columns were later published in two small books, *Heritage in Buckskin* and *Heritage in Buckskin, Volume Two*.

Smith founded the International Storytelling Center in Jonesborough, Tennessee, when in 1973, as a local journalism teacher, he hosted the first National Storytelling Festival. He was trying to find a way to share the beautiful stories of the area with the world and wanted to help save his dying Jonesborough through a rebuilt economy. The Storytelling Festival has done both. Due to his efforts, Jonesborough is the Storytelling Capital of the World.

In 1975, Jimmy Neil Smith founded the National Association for the Preservation and Perpetuation of Storytelling, which became the International Storytelling Center. Downtown Jonesborough now houses the headquarters, with a facility that storytellers from around the world strive to appear at to share their own stories.

Smith has served his community as a journalist, teacher, author, volunteer, businessman and restauranteur, and he was mayor for three consecutive two-year terms, beginning in 1978.

Introduction

I do not purport to say the counties represented here are the only counties in the greater Tri-Cities area, nor that they are the most important counties in this area; however, the information on iconic restaurants in these counties was more readily available than in others. Also, even if I had the time needed to write on every restaurant that our citizens hold dear, the book would run into thousands of pages. So, I have made every effort to include as many as possible. If you find yourself asking, "Why didn't she include [place restaurant name here]? It was the best restaurant in the area," please let me know, so a newer edition, or second book, can be more complete.

I have arranged the restaurants by type, including Drive-Ins; Burger Joints, Barbecue and Diners; Night Life and Grills; Drugstores; Upscale and More; and Cafés and Restaurants. However, there are a few that could have fit under more than one of the titles, so I chose what I considered to be the most relevant of the available groupings. In each group, the restaurants are arranged alphabetically.

During this process, I learned that there is little available historical information on restaurants, past and present. Historians from more than one area have expressed their desire to have such a resource in their collections. I have worked hard to include as many as possible from the past, but we have some really great restaurants still in business that this book would not be complete without.

Histories of the Counties

The greater Tri-Cities area has many counties in its grasp. The counties represented in this book are vital to our community, but so are many others around the area. Included in the greater Tri-Cities area are Scott, Wise, Lee, Russell and Washington Counties in Virginia and Carter, Greene, Hancock, Hawkins, Johnson, Sullivan, Unicoi and Washington Counties in Tennessee. The Tri-Cities is so named for Kingsport, Tennessee; Bristol, Tennessee/Virginia; and Johnson City, Tennessee.

The Tri-Cities works nicely as one community with citizens moving about in careers and shopping. So, a tally of the three main cities' citizens can be helpful to show just how populated our Appalachian community is.

Founded in 1856 by Henry Johnson and incorporated in 1869, Johnson City's 2010 census population was 63,152. Kingsport was settled in 1771, and the 2010 population was estimated at 48,205. Bristol, Tennessee, incorporated in 1856, and Bristol, Virginia, incorporated the same year as Goodson, Virginia, respectively had populations of 26,702 and 17,835 in 2010. The entire Tri-Cities area's population is estimated to be just over 500,000.

Sullivan County, Tennessee

Sullivan County was founded in 1779, with an area of 430 square miles. It is the second-oldest county in Tennessee. When established, it was still part of North Carolina, though the land was part of what the state ceded to the federal government when North Carolinians ratified the U.S. Constitution. Locals then created the State of Franklin government with the intent of becoming the fourteenth state. It didn't, but the State of Franklin lasted from 1784 until early 1789.

The county is named for General John Sullivan, though he had no specific connection to the area. He was an Irish American general in the Revolutionary War, a delegate in the Continental Congress, governor of New Hampshire and commander of the Sullivan Expedition against Iroquois who had attacked American revolutionaries. George Washington appointed Sullivan as judge of the United States District of New Hampshire from September 1789 to his death on January 23, 1795. Sullivan County was known as the Little Confederacy during the Civil War, due to its high population of Confederate supporters—1,586 in favor and 627 against. However, the Tri-Cities population's loyalties were split during the war, and most current residents have ancestors who fought on both sides. There are many stories of fathers, sons or brothers meeting against one another in battle. Some turned and walked away, but others fought. The Civil War caused strife in the Tri-Cities for many years after the war.

Blountville

Blountville is the only county seat in Tennessee that is unincorporated. To protect the county seat, a law was passed to ban neighboring cities from annexing within so many miles of the county courthouse. Blountville, named for William Blount, was founded in 1795 and is 4.9 square miles. In 1782, James Brigham bought six hundred acres, and in 1792, he gave thirty acres to Sullivan County to form a county seat and a hotel. In 1795, the property was divided to create a town and set up the county seat. Blountville grew through those years as a farming community. On September 22, 1863, the four-hour Battle of Blountville left the Confederates retreating as they watched their courthouse burn to the ground. The courthouse was rebuilt and is now considered the Historic Courthouse. It is on Highway 126, and county offices fill its space, as a new, active courthouse was built about a half mile away on Blountville Bypass next to the jail.

Blountville is also known through the state as the home of Ron Ramsey. Born on November 20, 1955, Ramsey grew up on a farm and graduated from Central High School and East Tennessee State University. He founded Ramsey and Ramsey Land Surveyors in 1981, and then in November 1990, he founded Ron Ramsey and Associates Realtors and Auctioneers. He is well known in the land sales and auctioning community of the Tri-Cities. In 1992, he ran for his first political office and was elected to the general assembly as a member of the Tennessee House of Representatives. He strongly advocated that politicians should have their home phone numbers listed in the phonebook so constituents could easily contact one whenever a need arose.

In 1996, he was elected to the state senate. He was reelected in 2000, 2004 and 2008. With initial support from all Republicans and one Democrat, he was elected and remained the speaker of the state senate from 2007 until he retired from politics in 2017. In Tennessee, the speaker of the senate is granted the title of lieutenant governor of the state and is next in line if the governor's position is vacated. Ron Ramsey was the forty-ninth lieutenant governor. He was the first Republican speaker of the senate of Tennessee since 1869. He was the first Republican lieutenant governor, since the state adopted the rule to grant the title to the speaker in the same year.

Kingsport

Sullivan County's largest city, Kingsport, has a small area in Hawkins County limits. Kingsport, set up in blocks to be the model city, attracted locals who love that you can easily travel through the town on the streets that link together methodically. Moving from one area of town to another is quick and painless. The city blocks downtown crisscross like a checkerboard to accommodate businesses, restaurants, hotels and apartments. Older homes in the area have been repurposed as apartments in and around downtown Kingsport. There are restaurants that once adorned this small town that are missed and loved, and there are new restaurants sprouting up around town that hope to become as beloved to their customers as the ones before.

Kingsport was known as a cruising town. Until the last fifteen years or so, everyone cruised Kingsport. In later years, it was just Broad Street, but in the '50s and '60s, the cruise strip was much larger. Jerry Irvin said it well in his Facebook post concerning the drive-ins of town and how to cruise them. Irvin said, in part, that the "'ultimate cruise' would hit all the drive-ins in town including: Chucks, Beacon, Texas Steer, PAL'S, Blue Circle, Dutch Boy, Shoney's, and Dee's." Biff-Burger was also a popular place during the late '60s and '70s, but it was a little farther out than the first ones mentioned.

Speaking of cruising Broad, as we call it, a national treasure once cruised this legendary street in the heart of downtown Kingsport. In 1955, a Grand Ole Opry performance came to Kingsport. It included an unknown new age rock 'n' roll singer named Elvis Aaron Presley (1935–1977). There were reportedly fewer than 600 people out of a possible 1,200-person capacity at the Civic Auditorium. The vast majority were die-hard country music fans. Elvis rocked the house, as always, and then moved into the hallway for autographs as the main event took the stage. He then took a few teenage girls out to his 1955 Cadillac convertible to show off a bit. It was there that history changed for one young lady and her not-so-happy boyfriend.[1]

A shy young lady missed the meet and greet in the hall but still wanted an autograph from this up-and-coming star. Her friend Billie Mae Smith, who later married and became a Barker, walked right up to Elvis's car, interrupting the teenage banter, and said, "When you get through showing off your car, my friend would like your autograph." She then told him that she "didn't particularly want one for herself."[2] Smith ended up spending the evening with Elvis, at one point pulling up beside a car holding Wayne "Booge" Allen, who was her boyfriend. He saw her. He saw Elvis. He was mad. There sat his girlfriend with a long-haired, ridiculously cute stranger. However, the evening with Elvis continued, and at one point during the date, they ate at Jimmie's Steak House just off the corner of Memorial Boulevard and Center Street.

Elvis returned to the Tri-Cities on March 17, 1976. The first paragraph of Vince Staten's article the day after Elvis Presley rocked Freedom Hall in Johnson City read, "Don't kid yourself. You'd rather be Elvis Presley than Gerald Ford. Or Ernest Hemingway. Or Johnny Bench."[3]

J.D. Sumner and the Stamps Quartet was on stage first. Then, comedian Jackie Kane took the stage, joking that "Freedom Hall…seats 8,000 with parking for 400." Sweet Inspirations took the stage before the thirteen-piece band, Joe Bershel Las Vegas Hilton, set up to play with Elvis. Staten went on to say that once Elvis took the stage, the band could not be heard for the first line due to the screams of the young ladies in the audience.[4]

KINGSPORT WAS SETTLED IN 1771, chartered in 1822 and re-chartered in 1917, with just over fifty square miles of land. It was named for King's Port, which was from King's Boat Yard on the Holston River. The boatyard was found across from Netherland Inn, a popular place for travelers to spend the night in past years. The town was developed after the Revolutionary War on the forks of the North and South Holston Rivers. In the late 1700s, animals were drawn to the area then known as Salt Lick for the ancient mineral lick in town.

There are many communities in Kingsport that were once on their own. Kingsport has annexed much of what is now here. Kingsport would become the largest city by land in the Tri-Cities. Some of the communities that have become part of Kingsport are Lynn Garden, Bloomingdale, Colonial Heights and Sullivan Gardens.

Long Island on the Holston River was home to many of the Cherokee in the area, and Fort Robinson was built on the island, as well. However, when the Cherokee were forced off their sacred lands, they cursed the land, saying, "No man would find peace there."[5]

Long Island has a bit of history in that Long Island iced tea was created by a man who lived there. That's our story anyway. There are many tales of how Long Island iced tea was created, but the most popular story here is that two men simultaneously created the popular drink. Old Man Bishop in Kingsport and a bartender in Long Island, New York, created the potent treat with only minor differences in ingredients. There is a huge battle on the internet about who actually invented the drink, with people naming bartenders around the country. But I'm going to share a bit of the Tennessee version that I have heard all my life. During Prohibition, Old Man Bishop ran a still making illegal liquor. He became a legend to the locals who wanted an alcoholic drink that looked like regular sweet tea. They could sit on their front porches, have a drink and a laugh at the agents tasked with finding the stills in the area as they walked right by the bootleggers sipping "tea" on their front porch.

Old Man Bishop created the drink, but his son, Ransom Bishop, perfected it in the 1940s, when he was running his own still. He sold his alcohol to many of the local bars. The Click brothers, who owned Club 81, took the drink mainstream in the '40s. This was twenty-five to thirty years before the other claims of invention take place, but Baker did not have the luxury of advertising that he had perfected his father's drink, as it is difficult to take credit for something that is illegal.

Bristol

Bristol was incorporated in 1856 and includes just over twenty-nine square miles. The town, as well as its sister site of the same name in Virginia, was named after Bristol, England. It is the birthplace of country music, as recognized by the U.S. Congress since 1998, since the Carter Family from Hiltons, Virginia, and Jimmy Rogers both recorded in Bristol in July 1927. Maybelle Carter's daughter, June Carter Cash, married Johnny Cash, and they had a part in this community until their deaths. NASCAR's Bristol Motor Speedway is also located here.

Tennessee Ernie Ford was born in the back room of a small house on Anderson Street in Bristol. The original home was built in the early 1900s, but fire took it many years ago. It was later rebuilt, causing the home to be altered, including having aluminum siding over the imitation brick siding. The Tennessee Historic Restoration required the removal of that aluminum and the imitation brick siding. Then, the clapboard siding was repaired as needed. The birth room now stores memorabilia and is used as a workroom for the foundation. The rest of the house serves as meeting rooms.

Bluff City

I want to mention the small town of Bluff City. It has a police department and a post office, though it has fewer than two thousand residents. Incorporated in 1887, Bluff City went through many name changes. Beginning as Choate's Ford, it changed names several times and then during the Civil War it was called Zollicoffer after the Confederate general of the same name but went back to the name of Union after the war ended.

The town caused a bit of controversy when it installed traffic cameras on Highway 11E. The town claimed to have issued more than 1,500 tickets in the first six months. In 2017, the expected budget would have it receive $600,000, which would cover more than a third of its total yearly expenses.

However, in 2010, a Gray, Tennessee resident, Brian McCrary, bought the former police department website after police failed to renew it. McCrary went to GoDaddy to buy the domain, and he used it to post information about fighting camera tickets.[6] The police department had changed its email address and was not getting the notices that had been sent to remind the small town to update the domain registration. When the department noticed that it had lost control, officers assumed the site had been hacked. On learning otherwise, they were eager to get the website back, but negotiations to regain control of the domain name were unsuccessful. McCrary used the website to educate the community on how to avoid paying those tickets. The site is no longer active for any party.

Those cameras have generated more money than any other single endeavor by the small community. So much, in fact, that a few residents claim to have paid enough to rebuild roads on their own. Some in the community have become experts on avoiding the cameras—or at least how to avoid paying the tickets. The traffic cameras were turned off in 2020.

Washington County, Tennessee

The county seat for Washington County is Jonesborough—the oldest town in the oldest county in the state. The county was established in 1777, while Tennessee was still part of North Carolina. Johnson City is the largest city in Washington County. The county was named for the first president of the United States. Loyalties during the Civil War were divided, leading the county to be at odds for much of the conflict.

With help from the community, Jonesborough has many original buildings that have been restored through the years to create a downtown that is rich with history and beauty.

One of the most famous gentlemen from Washington County was Landon Carter Haynes. He was a Confederate senator, speaker of the Tennessee House of Representatives and editor of Jonesborough-based newspaper *Tennessee Sentinel*. He lived in what is now the Tipton-Haynes State Historic Site.

Colonel John Tipton, who established the aforementioned historic site in the 1780s, was a leader who fought the establishment of the State of Franklin, as he and many others preferred to stay loyal to North Carolina. The Battle of Franklin at Tipton's farm was fought by the two sides over the establishment of the State of Franklin on February 27, 1788.

Jonesborough

Founded in 1779, Jonesborough has been a town longer than Tennessee has been a state. It was named for Willie Jones, who supported North Carolina's quest to expand west. During the reign of the State of Franklin, Jonesborough was the capital. The town is small, with only 4.3 square miles, but it makes up for that with the many community-supported activities—storytelling being the most popular and the most profitable.

According to an article in the *Johnson City Press*, "The town of Jonesborough will also be celebrating 15 years of Tree City USA status. A Tree City USA community achieves that designation by meeting four standards of sound urban forestry management: maintaining a tree board or department, having a community tree ordinance, spending at least $2 per capita on urban forestry and celebrating Arbor Day."[7]

Johnson City

Located in three counties—Washington, Carter and Sullivan—Johnson City was founded in 1856 but was not incorporated until thirteen years later. It was named Johnson City because Henry Johnson was in the right place at the right time. The new railroad station was named Johnson's Depot due to location. It became a major railroad hub in the Southeast, as three railway lines crossed there. The Tweetsie Railroad (East Tennessee and Western North Carolina Railroad or ET & WNC) was a big asset to the area. It made trips through the mountains so locals and vacationers could enjoy the beautiful scenery of the area. Briefly, the town was called Haynesville, but that did not last long, and the town went back to being Johnson City.

The year after the Carters made their recording in Bristol, Columbia Records held a recording session for Fiddlin' Charlie Bowman in Johnson City. He became a national star. Blind Lemon Jefferson and others from the community also recorded here and became local celebrities.

During Prohibition, Johnson City was called Little Chicago because of its ties with bootlegging for Al Capone. A bar downtown named Capone's was apparently frequented by its namesake whenever he was in town. Capone would come south to buy illegal liquor and then distribute it throughout the North. It has been known for years that Capone had an upscale apartment in the city, and that business is now in the National Register of Historic Places.

Another interesting note about Johnson City is that its residents did not like carnivals and circuses to set up in their town, or rather, they did not like the types of people who came to town with them. According to one article, they went so far as to enact a tax to dissuade them from setting up in town. The town set up what was nicknamed the Barney Fife ordinance.[8] That ordinance is from the Johnson City Tennessee City Code and Charter. It states, "Calling for aid. Any member of the police force is hereby empowered to call to his assistance as many of the inhabitants of the city as may be necessary to aid him in making arrests and in preventing or quelling any riot, unlawful assembly or breach of peace; and all persons so called shall be subject to the orders of the policeman, while on the duty for which they were called. It shall be unlawful for any person to refuse or to not obey the orders of such policeman, when so called by him."[9]

It is also important to mention that East Tennessee State University is in Johnson City. This is the college from which Kenny Chesney graduated. The James H. Quillen College of Medicine trains most of the doctors and nurses in the area, and many healthcare workers train here and spread through the world to help others.

HAWKINS COUNTY, TENNESSEE

The county seat for Hawkins County is Rogersville. The county was founded in 1787, a few years after William Armstrong was granted the land and built Stony Point. In 1897, French king Louis Philippe visited Armstrong's estate. Named for Benjamin Hawkins, an American planter, political leader, U.S. Indian agent delegate to the Continental Congress and U.S. senator from North Carolina, Hawkins County became a major throughway for people traveling from east to west, as Highway 11W cut straight down the center of the county. However, when Interstate 81 opened, some areas of Hawkins County became like a ghost town. The towns lost income and suffered economically. Now, the county is rebuilding. Restaurants, grocery stores and more are coming to the area that is slowly growing west from Mount Carmel.

President George Washington appointed Benjamin Hawkins to be the general superintendent for Indian affairs, with responsibilities for the Native American tribes south of the Ohio River and the principal Indian agent to the Creek Indians. In this role, he learned the Muscogee language and lived with his common-law wife, Lavinia Downs, a Creek Indian, and their seven children. The Creek Indian community tried to pressure Benjamin Hawkins into marrying Lavinia Downs. In 1812, Hawkins thought he was near death, and he married Lavinia Downs so his children would be considered legitimate pursuant to the United States laws after his death. He was wrong, though, and lived on until 1816 as a married man.

Benjamin Hawkins built a large complex, or plantation, that included mills, lots of cattle and hogs and a trading post. This was on the Flint River in Georgia in 1796. Hawkins used primarily slave labor, and this is where he set up the Creek Agency as part of the federal government. The state protected areas, Kyle's Ford Wildlife Management Area and part of Bays Mountain Park, bring many visitors to the area each year.

Rogersville

The first courthouse was in Rogers' tavern on the public square. It was established in 1787. The post office, built in 1815, is still standing on the corner of Main and South Hasson Streets. The area was founded in 1789, and it was incorporated in 1903.

The town was named for Joseph Rogers, born in August 1764 near Cookstown, Ireland, to James and Elizabeth Brown Rogers. He married Mary Amis. Her father ceded land near Crockett Spring to the couple to make their home. The Amises had bought the land from Davy Crockett's grandparents, who settled in the area in 1775.

The Civil War ravaged the town as the Battle of Rogersville turned families against each other on November 6, 1863.

Tennessee's first newspaper, the *Knoxville Gazette*, was printed by George Roulstone in Rogersville for the first year and then moved to Knoxville, Tennessee. Roulstone had come to Rogersville at the bidding of the governor of the Southwest Territory, William Blount. Twenty-three years after the *Knoxville Gazette* began printing in Rogersville, John B. Hood published the *East Tennessee Gazette* in Rogersville. Within two years, many publications came about, including the *Railroad Advocate*, the *Calvinistic Magazine* and the *Hawkins County Republican*. In 1885, the newspaper the *Holston Review* was born. It is still printed under the name of the *Rogersville Review* to this day.

Many important people have ties to Rogersville. Governor Bill Haslam graduated from Rogersville High School; Congressman Bill Jenkins was from the area; Bob Smith, who played Major League baseball for the Chicago Cubs, Cincinnati Reds and Boston Braves, was from Rogersville; author Ruth Hale fought for women's rights here; and Confederate general A.P. Stewart, graduate of West Point, taught at Cumberland University and was president of the University of Mississippi.

Rogersville has one of the largest Fourth of July celebrations in the area. Our family has celebrated there many times, and we have great memories of it. I don't remember every entertainer, but I remember why we took every picture we have from those times. Heritage Days is the second full weekend in October in downtown Rogersville, and of course, there is the Rogersville Holiday Special, where the town offers tours of some of the decorated homes in the historic district before celebrating with a yule log ceremony at Courthouse Square.

Surgoinsville

A French Huguenot, Major James Surguine, founded the area, and it was then "incorporated in 1815 but forgot about it and did not function as an incorporated town until changes in state law provided for distribution of state tax funds to municipalities."[10]

SCOTT COUNTY, VIRGINIA

Gate City is the largest city and the county seat in Scott County, Virginia. In the 2010 census, there were 23,177 people living in the county. An act of general assembly formed the county in 1814, naming it for Winfield Scott, who was a general in the U.S. Army. He fought in the War of 1812, the Mexican-American War, the Civil War and in conflicts with Native Americans. He was the Whig Party presidential nominee in 1852 but was defeated.

The county's first settler was Thomas McCulloch in 1769. Daniel Boone was often in the area, as he commanded several of the local forts. There is also a small area of the county called Daniel Boone in his honor. Dungannon's Flanary Archaeological Site has been listed in the National Register of Historic Places since 1983. Ross Carter, author of *Those Devils in Baggy Pants*, told a story about the Eighty-Second Airborne during World War II and is buried in the area on U.S. Route 421.

Clinchport

Seventy residents live in Clinchport. It is a demanding municipality, though it is the smallest in Virginia. In the late 1980s, Michael "Mikey" Mullins was elected mayor. He was eighteen years old and still in high school at the time, making him the youngest mayor in the United States. David Letterman invited Mikey to New York City a few times to join him and have a tour of the city. Mikey was a cutup, and he loved his friends and family. I was lucky enough to be one of those friends. We lost him in 2019 to cancer.

Clinchport was named for the Clinch River, which it sits on, and at one time, it was a budding community. However, the river that flows gently by the town has not been a friend to the growth, as it floods at every opportunity. The flood of 1977 destroyed the growing community, leaving a shell of what could have been lying on the banks of the river.

Gate City

The county seat was established in 1815 and was, at that time, named Winfield in honor of General Winfield Scott of the War of 1812. The county also derives its name from General Scott. The main street was named Jackson Street in honor of then-soldier and future president Andrew

Jackson. In 1817, the town was renamed Estillville for Benjamin Estill, a local man who was important in forming the county.

The town was incorporated in 1892 and, as of 2010, had a population of just over two thousand in an area barely more than four square miles. Gate City became an important town when travelers moved from Big Moccasin Gap to the North Fork of the Holston River, as it offered a chance for farmers to sell goods, manage legal affairs and catch rides on passenger trains, wagon trains and coach lines. The railroad offered the opportunity to transport and receive goods. A log yard, an iron ore and a glass sand business were able to grow in the area of Clinch Mountain. It was also a hotbed for sales of locally manufactured goods, such as sleds, staves, harnesses and wood pumps.

By 1915, Gate City had two livery stables, a blacksmith, an ice plant, a casket shop, furniture manufacturers and a dentist office. By 1930, it had three movie theaters that drew crowds from as far away as Clinchport. In 1958, the Pilot Flying J service station/travel centers were started in Gate City. Around that time, businesses began losing customers due to Kingsport's easy access and industry.

Nickelsville

The population of this little Southwest Virginia town is 383 in an area just under a half mile. It was named for the Nickels brothers, who ran the local mercantile store. Two landmarks in the National Register of Historic Places are Bush Mill and Kilgore Fort House. Maybelle Carter, mother of June Carter Cash, was a bluegrass artist from Nickelsville. Ollan Cassell, a gold medal–winning sprinter at the 1964 Summer Olympics, was also from Nickelsville.

Weber City

In 2010, the population was 1,327 in 1.72 square miles. Incorporated in 1954 and originally called Moccasin Gap after the gap that U.S. 23 runs through, Weber City was named for a joke that stuck with the little area in Virginia. Local businessman Frank Parks Sr. heard the future name on the *Amon 'n' Andy* radio show during a skit involving the upscale real estate development of Weber City. As a joke, Parker erected a sign outside his service station on the main highway that read "Welcome to Weber City." By the time the town was incorporated, the area had been called Weber City by the locals for so long that the name was officially chosen for the town.

HILTONS AND MACES SPRINGS

Another spot in the National Register of Historic Places, since 2002, is the Fulkerson-Hilton House. The Carter family settled in the area when Alvin Pleasant Delaney Carter and Sara Dougherty married and made it their home. They are buried behind Mount Vernon Methodist Church. Alvin Pleasant and Sara's children ran the nationally acclaimed Carter Fold—a music hall that still opens every weekend for local and national talent to entertain locals, who love the dance floor in front of the stadium-type room. Of course, Johnny and June Carter Cash performed there regularly, but so have other talents, such as Marty Stewart.

LOCAL NEWSPAPERS

Other papers have come and gone through the years, but the *Times-News*, *Johnson City Press* and *Bristol Herald Courier* have been the major ones in the Tri-Cities.

Times-News is mentioned several times in these pages because it is the major newspaper distributed in six counties in the greater Tri-Cities region. It has been through name changes in the history of becoming a booming paper. *Kingsport Times* was first published on April 27, 1916, by founder and publisher Cy Lyle. R.D. "Bob" Kinkead was the editor of the weekly paper.

In 1919, *Kingsport Times* changed owners to Thomas H. Pratt and Isaac Shuman. These men had been employees of the *Bristol Herald Courier*, another major paper in the Tri-Cities. In this arrangement, Shuman was editor and Pratt was the general manager. The paper changed leadership again, with Pratt staying and adding Howard Long. During this leadership, the paper began delivering daily on October 1, 1924.

In 1938, some local businessmen bought the paper. C.P. Edwards Jr., an insurance executive, was the president of the new venture, and W.J. McAuliffe was the editor.

In 1944, the paper changed names to *Kingsport Times-News*. Then, in 2018, it underwent another name change to *Times-News* to become more regional. The owner was the Northeast Tennessee Media Group, which included *Kingsport Times-News*, *Johnson City Press*, Jonesborough's *Herald and Tribune*, Erwin's *Record* and *Mountain City Tomahawk*, with production of all at the *Times-News* location. On January 1, 2020, things changed again as a new company was formed. Now, *Times-News*, *Johnson City Press*, the *Erwin Record*, *Jonesborough Herald and Tribune*, *Mt. City Tomahawk* and NET360 are part of the new Six Rivers Media. David Rau is the CEO, Allen Rau serves as vice president and Madeline Rau is the secretary.

The other major newspaper in the area, *Bristol Herald Courier*, has an equally interesting history. In 1865, John Slack founded *Bristol News*, and in 1870, he founded the *Bristol Courier*, which became Bristol's first daily paper in 1888. In 1903, George Carter, founder of the Clinchfield Railroad, moved to Bristol and founded the *Bristol Herald*. Carter left the area in 1907, causing his paper to merge with the *Courier* to form *Bristol Herald Courier*, as it remains today. The Carter family mentions this paper in their 1934 song "I'll Aggravate Your Soul."

I

Drive-Ins

Life is uncertain. Eat dessert first.
—Ernestine Ulmer

BEACON DRIVE-IN

Kingsport, Tennessee

Beacon Drive-In started advertising for staff in the *Kingsport Times-News* on October 20, 1953. On October 27, an ad ran in this paper announcing that Beacon Drive-In Restaurant was open to the public. Genuine pit barbecue was promised to customers, and it delivered on that promise. Whether dining in the modern dining area or eating in your car, the Beacon Drive-In promised a delicious meal for a reasonable price.

On January 10, 1954, an ad invited the community to the "Grand Opening 'Hospitality Party'" to be held on Monday, January 11, where everyone could get "free Barbecued Ham Trays" (barbecued ham, coleslaw and hush puppies) all day and night long. Bill Harrell, owner of this restaurant, as well as both the Kingsport and Johnson City locations of the Texas Steer Drive-Ins, was pleased with the turnout and served approximately two thousand patrons. The manager, "Big Jim" Williams, served the guests "straight out of about the most modern and largest barbecue pit in the South," according to the *Kingsport Times-News* on January 13, 1954. The article goes on to explain that this pit is able to barbecue fifty hams or five hundred pounds of beef at one time.

Above: The popular Beacon Drive-In. *Courtesy Kingsport Archives.*

Left: Like a beacon signaling a celebration, the lit sign of the Beacon Drive-In in the night sky led patrons to a celebration of tasty food and fellowship. *Courtesy Kingsport Archives.*

During the first week of February 1964, Beacon Drive-In served Rath's U.S. Prime Steaks from Waterloo, Iowa, with French fries for two dollars per plate. It boasted that you didn't have to pay for your steak if you couldn't cut it with a fork. Year round, it served entrées such as southern fried chicken and sugar-cured ham and sides including asparagus spears, deviled eggs and whipped potatoes. It also had French bread and biscuits, milk, coffee, tomato juice, tea, orange juice and grape juice.

In mid-1955, Mr. and Mrs. W.P. Major began to operate the Beacon Drive-In, while Jim Williams continued to manage the restaurant. The new owners, Bill and Nell Major, had been in the restaurant business for many years before opening the drive-in, as they had previously owned and operated Center Street Restaurant and Major's Motel before selling all of their interests in the area and moving to Florida. After some time away, they decided they missed the area and the restaurant business, so they moved home and bought Beacon Drive-In.

Later, James and Dorothy Manley bought Beacon Drive-In. Unfortunately, on June 17, 1961, James William Manley and his wife, Dorothy Irene Holt Manley, died. The *Times-News* reported that it appeared to be a murder-suicide, and unfortunately, their bodies were found by their seventeen-year-old son after a day of summer school at Dobyns-Bennett High School. Both victims were in their mid-forties at the time of their deaths. The Manleys had come to the area from Rutledge about a year and a half before their deaths.

Toward the end of that same year, Jack Trayer and Carl Ault, both from Bristol, worked to improve the service of the drive-in restaurant. The two men bought only the business and the fixtures; Joe Groseclose owned the property.

BIFF-BURGER

KINGSPORT, TENNESSEE

Bruce Brane and Earl Brane started the very successful fast-food chain, with a name stating they were the "best in fast food" (BIFF), in 1956 in Clearwater, Florida. They offered franchises to proprietors in the eastern United States, and their restaurants started popping up from Florida to Canada.

Biff-Burger, the first fast-food restaurant on Stone Drive, came to Kingsport on July 9, 1964, with Ray Carpenter as manager and Harold

Biff-Burger promised to be the "Best in Fast Food." *Courtesy Kingsport Archives.*

Vaughn as vice manager. At some point, Mike Shelton became manager and stayed in the position until the end of the restaurant's tenure in the town.

Biff-Burger's ads for the grand opening boasted that it was "Kingsport's Newest Ultra-Modern DRIVE-IN, PARK 'N EAT ESTABLISHMENT!" It also said that Biff-Burger only sold 100 percent USDA imported western beef.

Although there is some debate whether or not the side street was still named B Street or if it was Eastman Road (as it is currently) by the time Biff-Burger was opened in '64, the grand opening flyers say that it is "conveniently located on Stone Drive at Eastman Road Intersection," so I believe that puts an end to the local debate. Still, it is not known if Eastman was still a dirt road at that time or if it was the four-lane paved road that was to come.

The burgers were broiled, never fried, with the Roto Broil that Bruce and Earl Brane designed, allowing the meat to broil on the top shelf while the toasting buns on the bottom level caught the juices off the meat. Once cooked, the meat was dipped in special tangy barbecue sauce before being passed to the customer.

During the first three days of opening, parents were lured in by the promotional gimmick of giving kids free cotton candy each afternoon from the "Biff Burger Band Wagon and Biffy the Clown." There were also free balloons, pocket protectors, litter bags and rain hats. One ad said that the now-iconic restaurant was open from "11 am to ?" daily, including Sundays, but another said it closed at 11:00 p.m. Sunday through Thursday and opened 10:00 a.m. to midnight on Friday and Saturday.

The restaurant gave away a free drink with a $0.30 purchase. Also, it gave away $100 each day during the three-day grand opening celebration, which I imagine was unheard of during that time. "Play ALARM," a sign read. "If you are making purchases at Window No. 1 and The Alarm Sounds… You win $5! 20 winners each day!" That was quite the win considering Biff-Burgers were only $0.15 each and a large shake was $0.30.

Other favorites from the restaurant were tater tots—the first in Kingsport—and Biff-Dogs, which were circular hot dog wieners that fit nicely on a hamburger bun. Coleslaw filled the circle to make a round slaw dog. Locals also loved to flip change into the fountain in the front and would listen to the radio on specific days and times to hear specials from local DJs.

Financial difficulties in the 1970s caused stores to slowly close. With their parent company out of business by 1976, franchise owners could no longer get their products, so they had no choice but to close their doors, and all but two were gone by 1980. Those two are still in business. The closest one to Kingsport, renamed Beef Burger in the 1980s, has loyal locals who still refer to the restaurant by the original name of Biff-Burger. It is at 1040 West Lee Street, Greensboro, North Carolina. The other one still in business is Biff-Burger at 3939 Forty-Ninth Street North, St. Petersburg, Florida, and boasts that it is the longest-operating bar in Tampa Bay. Sadly, the portable building in Kingsport landed in the Surgoinsville area near Volunteer High School in Hawkins County, and it has sat there empty for decades.

BURGER-CHEF

Kingsport, Tennessee

On July 20, 1962, the *Kingsport News* reported that the Commission approved plans for Burger-Chef drive-in, which was reported to be a big competitor to the newly built McDonald's on Fort Henry Drive. I remember Burger-Chef's hamburgers and can still taste them sometimes. That is one hamburger I will crave for my whole life.

According to How Stuff Works, Burger-Chef aimed to profit from the ideas that created McDonald's success in the '50s. And Burger-Chef sure gave McDonald's a run for its money—at the beginning, that is. The Indianapolis-based General Equipment Manufacturing Company decided to try its hand at cooking and peddling burgers and shakes. In 1958, it launched the Burger-Chef chain with broilers that could make eight hundred flame-broiled patties with a "cook-out" flavor per hour.

In Kingsport, Burger-Chef was found at the intersection of Lynn Garden Drive and Truxton Drive—caught in the Y-type meeting of the two roads. It opened in November 1962. It offered "open flame" broiled hamburgers. Of course, it also had French fries, milkshakes and many other foods that go with hamburgers.

In December of that first year, Santa made an appearance for three days at Burger-Chef, and free treats were available to patrons. You could also buy the triple treat (broiled hamburger, milkshake and French fries) for only forty-five cents. The three-day grand opening celebration was not until Wednesday, January 23, 1963.

The nationwide fifth anniversary was celebrated on Friday, May 3, and Saturday, May 4, 1963, and the famous fifteen-cent burgers only cost ten cents each. In June of that year, a free summer children's show was sponsored by Burger-Chef. It included a movie at the State Theater, prizes and cartoons.

In 1964, Burger-Chef introduced a treasure hunt in which stamps on a French fry bag could win you free triple treats, Chef-Burgers, French fries, milkshakes or fish sandwiches. Foremost Dairies created a specific shake formula for this chain. Foremost Dairies was founded by Verona, Pennsylvania native Paul E. Reinhold, and it became a legend in the business industries. Reinhold, who founded Reinhold Ice Cream in 1916, was the pioneer of "modern ice cream." He learned that he could use "industrial refrigeration techniques to freeze ice cream at a plant, considered the first of its kind in the nation." J.C. Penney invited Reinhold to Florida to direct an ice cream and dairy operation, so Reinhold moved to Jacksonville, and Foremost Dairies was born. The dairy got its unusual name from Penney's prize bull, Foremost.

In January 1966, the owners of Burger-Chef named Gary Church general manager of the Kingsport and Johnson City locations. The Kingsport business had bought Johnson City's location. Johnny Gibson managed the Kingsport location, while Joe Taylor managed the Johnson City site.

In the *Kingsport News*, Burger-Chef presented a promotion, saying, "Tuesday Night is Family Night, 4 P.M. to 10 P.M., Buy them by the Bag

Burger-Chef competed with McDonald's for years but eventually lost the race. *Courtesy Kingsport Archives.*

Full! Cook-outiest." Yes, the company called its burgers the "cook-outiest" burgers around. They went on to say that "cook-outiest" was the "best way to say Burger-Chef Hamburgers. Why? Because we cook out 100% pure beef hamburgers over open flames...about the same way you cook out in your own backyard. It's the best because it seals in all the natural juices and beefy goodness. It's the cook-outiest hamburger at Burger-Chef." With this ad the restaurant offered hamburgers for only ten cents.

As part of a community betterment activity, Burger-Chef, along with McDonald's, Pal's, Dairy Queen, Nick Nave's, the Texas Steer and Biff-Burger, supplied food to several hundred teens who made an attack on litter on the residential streets of Kingsport. This was organized by Teen, Inc.

Burger-Chef worked hard to include residents in a way that created a real love for the restaurants. It always sponsored events and created events of its own. In May 1969, the company gave away a free black angus calf to one lucky winner. Periodically through the years, it would give away tickets for local entertainment, such as movie tickets with the purchase of a burger.

In May 1971, the restaurant gave away two bicycles. The manager, Ray Gibson, was to have his daughter pull the tickets from the pile. She got stage fright, so Gibson asked someone else to do it. A man read the ticket and said it was his daughter. After investigating the ticket, it was learned that someone else had actually won the bike. Gibson made a plea to the family to return the bike, but Gibson feared that he would have to give away three bikes instead of two. It turned out that it was an honest mistake, so Gibson let the girl keep her bike and bought a third bike for the actual winner. The ticket that had her name on it was actually a third ticket drawn, but no one realized what had happened at the time.

In September 1971, Burger-Chef had a national program in which each person could order a book cover that highlighted how the Wild West was born. Adults could also cash in by getting a Wild West mural map. The company also gave away free Coke glasses, tempered for safety. Then in January 1972, it gave away a Willy Wonka candy bar and a golden ticket with every purchase. With the ticket and one dollar, you could buy a Willy Wonda's candy factory kit, which included nineteen different molds, three packets of decorations, forty-eight candy bar wrappers, stick-on labels, an instruction booklet and a decal sheet. There was no chocolate included. While some of the offers were only available with a purchase from the restaurant, many were available without a purchase.

Burger-Chef gave away its Book of Value in the spring of 1975 and called it "incredaburgable." The books were free with any $2.50 purchase and had more than $20.00 worth of coupons, refunds and discounts. Many of the local patrons made that $2.50 purchase to help with meals for their families.

Unfortunately, in 1981, due to declining profits, Burger-Chef restaurants were sold to Hardee's. Children all around can thank Burger-Chef for its one lasting legacy: Burger-Chef created the fun meal in 1973, which meant that a toy was included in the meals of a small hamburger, fries, drink and dessert. McDonald's jumped on that idea and created the Happy Meal that is still used today. Where the Burger-Chef restaurant once fed and entertained its community now sits a Dairy Queen, which is just as busy as Burger-Chef once was.

Campus Drive-In

Gate City, Virginia

Campus Drive-In has always been an integral part of the Scott County community. Proof rests in its day-to-day schedules. It has always welcomed the local students and clubs to meet in its dining room. I have been told that class reunions have even been planned there. It also allowed the local Jaycees to use the parking lot to install seat belts in cars back in the decades when they were not put in all cars during manufacturing. The Jaycees did this to help improve safety in their county.

Campus Drive-In was opened in the late 1950s by Darrell Dougherty. He had quite a life leading up to owning his own restaurant. After graduating from Nickelsville High School, he studied at Lincoln Memorial University. He was working for J.C. Penney in 1943, during its campaign to sell war bonds. After returning home, he was inducted into the armed forces in the late summer of 1945. He married Nancy Williams in 1947, and they had a child in September 1954.

Through the years, Dougherty served many roles in his community. He was chairman of the Gate City Jaycee Club, co-chair of the 1963 Children's Home Society of Virginia (with Billy Frazier), served various roles for the annual Tobacco Festival that took place in Weber City and was a councilman and served many years as mayor.

He helped make Legion Field a reality. The Gate City Blue Devils football team has been a powerhouse through the years, after winning its first state

The Campus Drive-In has always been a downtown Gate City favorite. In the 1960s, Gate City High School students were allowed to leave the campus for lunch, and many walked the .3 mile to get a good lunch. *Author's collection.*

championship in 1970. Locals worked hard to give them Legion Field. Dougherty and B.J. Broadwater were two of many who solicited donations in honor of completing the field. Then, on July 25, 1966, season passes for the high school football games went on sale at Campus Drive-In. These seats guaranteed a reserved spot in the stands for only six dollars per person.

CHUCK'S DRIVE-IN

Kingsport, Tennessee

According to various news reports, Chuck's Drive-In started at 1649 West Sullivan Street but, at some point, moved to 840 Industry Drive. The owner, Wesley Dykes, also owned East End Drive-In on U.S. 11W in Rogersville. He enjoyed engaging the public with contests. One such contest was to give away a pony at 5:30 p.m. on Labor Day of 1962. During these contests, people could enter to win at either location, but one prize was given. Another contest in 1961 led Dykes to give away tickets to win a Thunderbird.

The East End Drive-In property was auctioned off in 1977 by Johnson-Johnson and Associates, a real estate and auction company. The property included a ten-unit East End motel, the office and contents, East End Drive-In and service station, an eight-unit mobile home park and five mobile homes, catering trucks, reach-in coolers, a riding lawn mower, a boat and many other things.

Chuck's Drive-In remained open through the 1990s. In its heyday, the drive-in was open twenty-four hours per day and offered a delivery service. I often hear people say that they would love to have a hamburger from Chuck's.

DAIRY CUP

Mount Carmel, Tennessee

Dairy Cup has been a beloved stop for fifty years, primarily due to the love of community that the original owner, Hobert "Skip" Smith, displayed in his efforts to be a positive role in local children's lives. Skip and his wife, Jimmie, founded Dairy Cup in 1969.

Skip Smith owned Dairy Cup in Mt. Carmel. *Author's collection.*

Just across the tracks from Mt. Carmel Elementary School, Dairy Cup was a vital part of school celebrations. Skip would bring coolers of ice cream for field day, and he and his wife would hand out goodies to the students. The local ball teams were awarded a free ice cream after a game. Those kids' parents were loyal to Skip, and the kids grew up and took their own families to Dairy Cup. Skip loved his people. He would meander through the diner and talk to customers who were friends. He would learn your name, who your parents were, where you went to school and what your dreams were.

Skip had a few burglaries through the years. Once, someone broke in and stole change from the cigarette machine and jukebox, as well as ten pounds of cheese. Another burglar took a "great deal of hamburger," according to Skip.

Skip and Jimmie were always willing to help. When my classmate and friend Brian Hoskins died suddenly just weeks after graduation, Skip and Jimmy stepped in to aid the family. He was encouraging and loving, and we were all sad when he sold Dairy Cup and decided to retire.

Dairy Cup still offers the community the same service and love as it did when Skip was the owner. It still offers burgers (including a veggie burger), hot dogs, BLTs, egg sandwiches, specialty sandwiches, fries, tater tots, onion rings, crunchies, fish, soup and salad, beans, cakes, parfaits, fifty-five shake flavors and lots and lots of ice cream flavors and dishes. To drink, you can get JFG coffee, milk and all Pepsi products.

Skip did not like retirement, so he opened Skip's Diner in 1997 on the corner of Main Street and Kaywood Avenue in Mt. Carmel. Then, he opened SKIPEZ Market on the corner of Main Street and Hammond Avenue. In 2009, he opened what would be his last endeavor. Skip's Diner in the Allendale community of Kingsport (in the small area where Kingsport falls in Hawkins County) was meant to have the original menu of Dairy Cup—hamburgers, hot dogs and ice cream. However, there were customers who had followed Skip for years. So, when a loyal customer would request an item, Skip would add it to the menu.

Each time Skip changed venues or retired, he did so due to having a heart attack. He would have a heart attack and decide that he needed to retire and would do so. Then, he would feel the "call of the restaurant business" and open another location. Hobert "Skip" Smith died in March 2019. His family closed the diner, and his wife, Jimmie, and their daughter, Charity, were left to remember him.

DIXIE QUEEN DRIVE-IN

Rogersville, Tennessee

The popular Dixie Queen Drive-In was co-owned by Warren Ray Kirkpatrick. He also managed the restaurant.

DUTCH BOY DRIVE-IN

Kingsport, Tennessee, and Weber City, Virginia

Dutch Boy Drive-In sat at 1753 Fort Henry Drive in Kingsport, where the Asian Market now sits. This corner of Fort Henry Drive and Eastman Road has been a convenient location for business in Kingsport for many years. This drive-in boasted that it was the "Home of the Broasted Chicken." Dutch Boy Drive-In was co-owned by Pastor Nick Nave and F.C. "Red" Lowery.

In Weber City, Dutch Boy Drive-In sat at the North Fork of the Holston River. I was told that the owners of the two locations were likely the same; however, one person told me that Garland Smith owned them. According to research mentioned in chapter 3 under Cavalier Grill, this location was part of a police force sweep of gambling devices on location.

ELMS DRIVE-IN AND RESTAURANT

Gate City, Virginia

The Elms Drive-In and Restaurant was owned by Bob and Shirley Greenwell. The drive-in was in West Gate City on the Big Stone Gap Highway.

FROZEN CUSTARD DRIVE-IN

Nickelsville, Virginia

Frozen Custard Drive-In was nestled in the Nickelsville area of Scott County. The drive-in sat on a one-third-acre corner lot in the heart of the Southwest Virginia industrial town. The building was ten thousand square feet and had a rocked driveway. The yearly estimated payroll for the drive-in was $7 million. In 1953, the owner had a heart attack and was forced into retirement. He sold his beloved drive-in at that time.

HOB-NOB DRIVE-IN

Gate City, Virginia

Hob-Nob is a staple in the greater Tri-Cities area—one that everyone seems to know about, and each person has their personal favorite on the menu. Mine is the slaw dog. It has just the right amount of fresh, delicious slaw on top of a delicious dog. But that's not all. Its hamburgers are delectable, and the home-cooked meals are on the top of many patrons' lists of must-haves. But how did the Hob-Nob Drive-In get its name? According to an article by Fred Sauceman, a stonemason laying block for the new building in 1952 said, on discovering he was building a restaurant, "You're going to have a hob-nob of a good time." And a name was born.[11]

The owner, Ross Jenkins, earned a business degree from Emory and Henry College in Southwest Virginia. He arrives at the drive-in at 4:15 a.m. each day to open the restaurant. He chops, cuts, peels and preps all of the food for that day. With all he does each morning, he is often not done when it is time to open. But open he must, as at 11:00 a.m., people are already lined up at the door.

When I went to visit, I held back to give others time to enter so that I could have a moment to let Ross know I was there. He was still prepping and needed a few minutes to finish, so I went to a table with two seats and waited patiently for him. As I looked around the dining room, I saw that there were only a few booths available. I was sitting at the only table with chairs, and the rest of the seating was in booths that sat four adults. There was, however, one booth that sat eight adults.

Left: The Hob-Nob Drive-In sign excites patrons as they travel north from Gate City. *Author's collection.*

Right: Hob-Nob founders Mr. and Mrs. Strong. *Courtesy Ross Jenkins.*

Ross was soon ready, and we were able to chat. He employs twenty people, none of whom are family. This surprised me, as the drive-in started as a family business with his grandparents nearly seventy years ago. He made the decision to not hire family a long time ago because family members sometimes feel as though they deserve the best breaks or special days off when the reality is often the opposite. Owners often expect family to step in when times are tough, so Ross decided to not hire family to avoid any issues around the business. He also discussed the difficulties of employing family during important times in people's lives. If half of your staff is family, a business will sometimes have to close for a funeral, holiday celebration or wedding.

But things sure did not start out that way. When Ross's grandparents, Bent and Elgia Strong, opened Hob-Nob in the early 1950s, it was a family affair. Ross remembers spending summers with his grandparents. His uncle was always in the kitchen. There was a chair in the corner, and that's where you would find Ross watching the hustle and bustle of feeding a community with love and appreciation. Ross's grandmother would load him up with a bag of chocolate candy from the front counter, and Ross was allowed to play in the back alleyway that wrapped around the building. Of course, he had to watch out for cars, as they would often drive around the building to get a better parking spot.

The small parking area is adequate for the business. There was once an area where two cars could park under an awning, but Ross got rid of that many years ago to allow spaces for two more cars in the lot. He says that after years of standing there, the awning needed major repairs that were not worth the time or money. He also has chosen to have the door on that side of the building as an emergency exit only. He was having problems with customers lining up at the front door waiting for a booth and someone would come in the back door and grab an empty one before the next in line could be seated. However, if Ross has a customer who is disabled or ill and cannot make the walk around, he will open the door for easier access.

Ross was not born in Southwest Virginia. He lived in Kentucky and North Carolina as a child. When he agreed to inherit Hob-Nob, he told everyone that he was moving back to Gate City until a cousin pointed out he had never actually lived in the area. But in his heart, he knew he was moving back to Gate City because this quaint tiny town had always been home.

The Strongs' home was next door to the drive-in, and in 1966, a tractor trailer spun out of control and crashed into the front of their home. According to the *Kingsport News*, the Strongs were not in the home at the time, but Bent Strong's niece Judy Alley and her mother, Mrs. Ada Alley, actually were, and they said the crash sounded like a freight train barreling through the front door. The truck driver said that an oncoming car had "crowded him off the highway."

In 2018, it was no surprise that Hob-Nob won the Best Burger award from the Southern Virginia Reader's Choice competition. My paternal grandparents lived about a mile from Hob-Nob, and my sister and I always angled for a trip to our favorite restaurant. We ate there so often, and during such happy times, that a trip to Hob-Nob on Daniel Boone Road feels like going home.

TEXAS STEER DRIVE-IN

KINGSPORT, TENNESSEE

Due to conflicting information in advertisements, there are some questions as to the exact address of the Texas Steer Drive-In. Some state that the address was 420 West Center Street and others say the number was 520. What is known is that it was on the corner of West Center and Clinchfield Streets in Kingsport. This location later housed the Appalachian Credit Union and is now the location of Berry's Pharmacy. The number address of this location is now 460.

In November 1950, the drive-through opened with an invitation to the whole city to attend. It boasted that it served PET ice cream and milk exclusively. The full menu included a chicken breast, drumsticks or short leg chicken with fries and all the trimmings for sixty-five cents; genuine pork barbecue for thirty-five cents; a hamburger for twenty-five cents; onion rings for twenty-five cents; coffee or tea for ten cents; milkshakes or malt shakes for twenty-five cents; and milk and soft drinks for ten cents. The specialty was the Texas steer sandwiches, which featured the "finest meat money could buy," according to an ad in the *Kingsport Times-News* at opening in November 1950.

Curb girls were the waiters of the day. They would go out to the "curb" in the parking lot—each parking space—take orders and return with food for the entire car. They worked hard but had a lot of fun too. Fountain girls made the drinks for the curb girls to pass out.

The restaurant was also called the Texas Steer Family Restaurant. It would prepare picnic lunches for patrons to pick up.

An exciting event in Kingsport was reported in the *Kingsport Times-News* on May 20, 1956. The ad described a giveaway of a free car: "To be given away free! Labor Day, September 3rd, This beautiful new 1956 Metropolitan will be given away absolutely free Labor Day, September 3rd! Come In and Ask for Details…Texas Steer Drive-In, 520 W. Center St., Phone CI 5-9577." Another ad in October 1958 said, "Don't leave TV—call me for fast delivery service, dial CI 5-9577, Jimmy Pepper's Texas Steer Family Drive-In, Open 'til 1 a.m. except Sat. & Sun. 2 a.m., Delivery Service Charge 25 cents."

On July 28, 1960, an ad in the *Kingsport Times-News* reported, "Another current national trade publication, *Drive-In Management*, carries a couple of pictures and a page story on a recent promotion idea at Kingsport's Texas Steer Drive-In."

These promotion ideas were: "Texas Steer, according to co-owner Jimmy Pepper, had averaged selling $576 in cheeseburgers per weekend. Pepper arranged to set up a contest among his 'car hops.' He had each hostess wear a corsage made up of $2 bills.

"Whenever a customer asked the girl about her unusual corsage, she would tell him about the cheeseburger contest. The result: 1,729 cheeseburgers were sold during the weekend, representing an overall business increase of $1,000."

The Steer, as it was affectionately called by local patrons, was known to donate to worthy causes. It would donate food or drinks to organizations that would have to watch pennies to meet their agendas.

"Our hamburgers are the largest in town," claimed the Texas Steer management—owner and co-managers Fred Shoemaker and his wife, Velma. Fred once said that the meat used for the hamburgers was the best choice beef available to the area. "One of our hamburgers is practically a meal in itself," he said proudly. The younger generation would pile into the parking lot after leaving a movie or sporting event in Kingsport. Many who were cruising Broad Street would delight in arriving at the Texas Steer for one of the legendary hamburgers or milkshakes. Speaking of milkshakes, it offered not only chocolate and vanilla but also strawberry, pineapple, banana, peanut and others. Malts were also on the favorites list.

Even families loved to go to the Steer. It was a great way to go out to eat without having to get dressed up in fancy clothes to be presentable to friends and neighbors, as they could stay in their own vehicles and get curb service. Menus were found at each of the sixty stalls in the parking lot and included sandwiches and shakes among other options. There was an intercom that led directly to the kitchen for patrons to order. In a few minutes, one of the restaurant's courteous curb girls would deliver their order to their car. The favorites of the young patrons were a giant hamburger with a peanut soda. However, parents were varied in their choice of food and beverage.

For those who preferred to dine inside, there was a large dining area. There were always daily specials offered. Meatloaf, southern fried chicken, beef, pork and turkey and dressing—to name a few—were always on the menu, along with juicy steaks and a broad choice of seafood.

Texas Steer served breakfast until 11:00 a.m. each day, and patrons could always expect to find hot biscuits and gravy, bacon and eggs, ham and many other items.

As long as a customer met the minimum order financially, Texas Steer would deliver to local addresses with no added charge. It opened at 5:30

a.m. each weekday and closed at 1:00 a.m. Sunday through Thursday. On Friday and Saturday, it stayed open until 2:00 a.m.

In 1968, there was an article in the paper about some boys being arrested for drinking in the parking lot, but the Steer was not mentioned again until there was an article in *Kingsport Times-News* stating that the restaurant was no longer open. The August 9, 1975 article discussed the history of jukeboxes and said, in part, "Gone are the Beacon Drive-In, Shorty's Drive-In, the Dutch Boy, Golden Dip, Indian Drive-In, the Del Mar, and the Texas Steer. Chuck's Drive-In has survived but it's gone through management changes and it's a different type crowd." Less than two years later, the used car department of Kingsport Motors moved onto the lot where the Texas Steer once was. Clinchfield Street was opened through to Stone Drive in the early 1970s, which created a major artery into downtown. This helped Kingsport Motors, which was celebrating its sixth anniversary, make the decision to move its lot to that location.

The area was booming for a few years, and then activity stalled downtown. Most of the big businesses had moved to Stone Drive or Fort Henry Mall, and those left downtown were struggling. Kingsport Press and Mead Co. were on the corners of Clinchfield and Center Streets, as they had been for many years, and farther down Clinchfield was a grocery store, the main throughway to Holston Valley Medical Center and the entrance to Kings' Giant Plaza, which was on the corner of Clinchfield Street and Stone Drive. All of that has since closed. There is now a medical building, a grocery store and a farmer's market sitting where the Press once was. Domtar is now at the old Mead location. Another medical plaza is where Kings' Giant Plaza once was, and a new upscale apartment building is where the grocery store once sat.

The only time to eat diet food is while you're waiting for the steak to cook.
—Julia Child

II

Burger Joints, Barbecue and Diners

Ask not what you can do for your country. Ask what's for lunch.
—Orson Welles

A&W RESTAURANT

KINGSPORT, TENNESSEE

A&W Restaurant was named for the owners, Roy Allen and Frank Wright, and in 1925 became the "first franchise restaurant in America."[12] On A&W Restaurant's website, it lists accomplishments for the franchise through the years, including that in 1999, "in conjunction with A&W's 80th Anniversary, the world's largest Root Beer Float was created." The spectacular float used "2,562.5 gallons of Root Beer" and broke the world record.[13]

The local franchise was owned by Gerald and Joanne Kleven. Their son, Dan Kleven, managed the restaurant. Dan's wife, Sue, worked with my mother, and they are friends to this day. Sue once gave my children miniature A&W root beer mugs left from the family's time with the restaurant.

BANTAM CHEF

Weber City, Virginia

Burgers, hot dogs, fries, shakes and cones—Bantam Chef owner Jerry Elliott operated the beloved restaurant on Highway 23 north of Weber City. Although it was a chain business, when it opened in Weber City, locals were excited and flocked to the new restaurant. The chain had locations in Georgia, North Carolina, South Carolina and Virginia at the time. The first Tennessee restaurant was found in Rogersville next to the Hawkins Elementary School. It opened on November 3, 1976. Like many restaurants of that time, it did not open until noon on Sunday. Brenda Massingill shared with me via the Facebook group "Scott County Virginia Places, Faces, and Memories," she remembers "Virgie Roberts homemade fried pies" that she could purchase at Bantam Chef.

BURGER BAR

Rogersville, Tennessee

Burger Bar was on the corner of Church and Main Streets in downtown Rogersville. Rubel Price owned this location as well as the Tennessean Restaurant and Motel. Lots of locals had something to tell me about this local eatery. They communicated their thoughts to me through the Facebook group "You Might Be from Hawkins County If…"

Christa Greene said, "I remember all the old men would sit at the bar and smoke!"

David Newberry said of Granny, a female employee who answered to that name, "Granny that worked there was my mammaw."

And Stephen Hyder said that the restaurant was "where O'Henry's is now. One half of the building (where the big dining room is) was John's Barber Shop. The corner where the Burger Bar was, had large plate glass windows where the walls are now."

DIXIE BARBECUE

Johnson City, Tennessee

Alan Howell had quite a successful career in the restaurant business. He started as a young man working at Skoby's in Kingsport. After many years of service with the Barger family, Alan went into business for himself. His business detailing cars ended when he decided to get back into the restaurant industry. He owned and operated Richard A's near East Tennessee State University until it became more of a stop for late-night drinks than noontime hamburgers. He told me that he was getting too old to be there early enough to get the store ready to serve lunch and then be up all night with the partying college kids too. He then opened Dixie Barbeque at 3301 North Roan Street. This barbecue restaurant was in service for twenty-eight years before closing on December 31, 2015.

Alan Howell appreciated his start in the business. On the back wall of Dixie Barbecue, Alan hung memorabilia from his time at Skoby's. On the menus, there were several choices of barbecue and a list of the things that were true, labeled "yes," and that were not true, labeled "no." On the yes list was "I DID work at Skoby's for nearly 10 years"; "That music IS 'beach music,' a southern specialty"; and "Let's 'shag'—we have it for sale too!" referring to the 1960s shag music Alan played in the restaurant. On the no list was "Michigan, Penn State, and Ohio pennants will NOT be found here" and "Swine will NOT be served before its time."

When I sat down with Alan in his home to discuss his career, he shared that the best times of his life were centered on food. In fact, he signed off on the long-winded menus at Dixie Barbecue by saying, "I've been feeding the Tri-Cities for nearly 35 years. This is the most fun I've had yet. Come Join Me! I'm serious about barbeque—how about you? —Alan Howell."[14]

At Dixie Barbecue, Alan created many of his own sauces from scratch. He would travel to other restaurants that had reputations for good barbecue, and he would sample what they had. He would reproduce from taste but added his own flair. He created his seven famous sauces by adding a little of something here and taking away something else there. Alan was featured in many articles and books throughout the years, including the *Johnson City Press* and *Southern Living*. Hungry customers came from all over the world. He noted that he was shocked when someone from Australia visited. He also had customers from Germany, Japan and Tasmania. He always loved when someone from another country would visit and rave

Above: Another college student favorite was Poor Richard's. ETSU students would grab a beer and relax after hours in this great spot. *Author's collection.*

Left: Dixie Barbecue was successful at this location, but Nick's extension of the Kingsport restaurant did not have much luck. The building still sits empty. *Author's collection.*

about his barbecue, and he loved it even more when they were return customers, of which he had several.

I asked Alan if he had any problems over the symbol of the Rebel flag and the flags he flew in the restaurant. He smiled and paused before saying, "Not until those last few months when it became a national hot spot." He shared that customers said little against the flag, and most of those comments were to ask him to carry merchandise donning the Rebel flag. However, he did receive a little national attention in the form of some newspeople contacting him from other places, but he does not know of anyone trashing the reputation of his restaurant or his own person publicly. He said that he simply saw it as a sign of southern pride, like a Tennessean might fly a state flag to show pride.

Alan, not in his best health, is retired now and lives in his home in Johnson City with his family. His years in the restaurant business fill his memories with happiness.

FRONT PORCH STORE AND DELI

Fort Blackmore, Virginia

The Front Porch Store and Deli on the Clinch River Highway in Fort Blackmore, Virginia, had many functions. It had great catfish, burgers and fries, but it was also a type of convenience store. It sold just about anything a person could want. For example, it had perfume, fishing licenses, a bear weigh-in and a deer weigh-in for those who would hunt bears in the area.

GREG'S PIZZA

Johnson City, Tennessee

Everyone I talked to in the Johnson City area said that I must include Greg's Pizza. It is found near the Johnson City mall, where there are many restaurants on Roan Street. It is one block off the main throughway on Broyles Drive, and there is a second location on Elk Drive in Elizabethton.

In Johnson City, *the* pizza place for most is Greg's Pizza. *Author's collection.*

It has been offering gourmet pizzas, homemade pasta and subs for more than fifty years. The chefs will even prepare a pizza that you can cook later at home.

Greg Campanello is the founding father of Greg's Pizza. He began with a pizza place in Elkhart, Indiana, called Volcano Pizza, which is still in business and is owned by Greg's son, Fritz, and his wife, Michelle. The owners of the local Greg's Pizza restaurants are Eddy and Cindy Zayas-Bazan.

Home Sweet Home and the Mezzanine Tea Room

Kingsport, Tennessee

I have heard wonderful things about the Mezzanine Tea Room, primarily from my own mother. She ate there often with friends from work. They would take a meeting to the tearoom so they could grab lunch on a busy day. The tearoom was nestled in a gift shop at 122 Broad Street. The small business closed before I had the opportunity to dine there, but owner Sharon Hurd sold a few of the teapots used in the shop. My mother bought a few to sell in her own bookstore, and they sold quick. Sharon's daughter, Deana, owns LuLu's Tea Room in Powell, Tennessee.

INDIAN BARBECUE

Kingsport, Tennessee

Many restaurants have been more popular among certain groups of people, and Indian Barbecue on Center Street was no different. Local author Barbara Goodlett devoted an entire chapter of *A Quarter's Worth of Love* to this popular teenager hangout. Students from Dobyns-Bennett High School loved that their beloved Indian logo was on the front of the "square, flat-topped building with plain old asbestos siding and two big front windows."[15]

According to Goodlett, Indian Barbecue "was glamorous, exciting, [and] almost off-limits to anyone who wasn't popular, pretty, an all-round great guy or a jock." A nickel jukebox played song after song as long as patrons continued to feed it coins.

"O.P Harp, Indian Barbecue, 1104 Bristol Highway, Kingsport" was issued a federal gambling tax stamp on Thursday, December 6, 1951.[16] According to an article in the *DePaul Law Review*, the Kefauver Crime Investigation Committee, in the Revenue Act of 1951, created two laws: bookmakers and lottery operators were required to pay a 10 percent "excise on all wagers concerning sporting events or lotteries" and a fifty-dollar-per-year occupational stamp tax.[17]

In 1962, Lula Grills, owner of Indian Barbecue, was fined $10 "for operating a business without a special privilege license."[18] Then, in 1964, "Judge Marvin Parsons fined Mrs. Max Bower $5 after she pleaded innocent…but admitted three youths…ages 13, 15, and 16 were playing the [pinball] machines" at the restaurant.[19]

L.E. CLARK GROCERY

Kingsport, Tennessee

In the early 1970s, L.E. Clark Grocery opened on South Wilcox Drive (Highway 93) in the Vernon Heights community of Sullivan Gardens, now a subsection of Kingsport. The grocery was a restaurant that would be a beloved part of the model city for many years to come. In fact, the restaurant was owned and operated by the same owner until 2019, when the doors closed for good. The grocery carried staple groceries, quality meats, fresh fruits and vegetables and other produce. It had everything you might need to prepare for a good home-cooked meal. The short-order menu of burgers and more was available Monday through Saturday from 8:00 a.m. to 10:00 p.m. and on Sundays from 12:00 p.m. to 10:00 p.m.

PAL'S SUDDEN SERVICE

Kingsport, Tennessee

Pal's, as locals call the successful and unique fast-food restaurant in the Tri-Cities area, is "one of America's leading quick-service restaurant chains," according to the Pal's Sudden Service website.[20]

In fact, it is the "first restaurant chain in the country to earn the Malcolm Baldrige National Quality Award." The National Institute of Standards and Technology, a division of the U.S. Department of Commerce, presents these awards to businesses with the "highest level of national recognition for performance excellence that a U.S. organization can receive."[21]

Pal Barger and his late wife, Sharon, own this chain of restaurants that are only found within a short distance of the headquarters on Konnarock Road in Kingsport. My sister and her daughter worked at Pal's for several years, so I had the opportunity to meet many of the employees through the years. I also had the immense pleasure of meeting Pal's daughter, Chris, when she was running the Gate City branch.

The drive-throughs are all painted bright colors with large renditions of the food they serve donning the front of the restaurant. The Lynn Garden location has a larger-than-life man, formerly the Michelin Man, holding a hamburger towering over the walk-in and take-out restaurant.

A few naysayers have expressed through the years that they would not eat in a restaurant that they were not able to go into and inspect, but they have no standing. Pal's restaurants are as clean as a restaurant could possibly be, as they have rigorous cleaning schedules. I once heard that Pal said he would never have a restaurant so far away that he could not drive to it and give a detailed surprise inspection, at least a four-hour tour and then head back home in one day. He would never have a restaurant that he could not ensure was following guidelines.

Pal and Sharon Barger have had many ventures in the restaurant business. For some time, Sharon's Barbeque operated in downtown Kingsport. I

The beautiful sun illuminating Pal's. *Courtesy Pal's Sudden Service.*

Joining the peculiar style of the drive-through restaurants, Pal's Sudden Service Headquarters creates a space for creativity and joy. *Author's collection.*

Pal's Bucks are the restaurant's gift certificates. *Author's collection.*

Left: Pal Barger believes in honoring his country with a large flag in front of every location. *Courtesy Pal's Sudden Service.*

Below: Sharon's Barbecue, found downtown, was owned by Sharon Barger, Pal's wife. *Courtesy Kingsport Archives.*

have heard that there were burgers mixed with caviar, but I never had the opportunity to taste it myself. Like the Pal's restaurants, Sharon's place had a larger-than-life attention getter—the front half of a car was used as an awning over the front door.

PRATT'S BARBEQUE

KINGSPORT, TENNESSEE

The layout of Pratt's Barbeque is unique, and it was designed to be so. What architect Larry Poole created in the 1970s was dubbed "Pratt's Barn." But it didn't begin as that.

Honest John Barker and his wife, Mable, ran a restaurant in Kingsport in one end of a building. On the other end was a souvenir and gift shop. A small, apartment-type dwelling for the Barkers was also in the building. During his time in business, Honest John carved what he called the "Big Indian." In 2018, its neck broke, and Pratt's had extensive work done to repair the thirty-two-foot-tall structure.

Honest John's showing the "Big Indian" that owner John D. Barker carved. *Author's collection.*

Pratt's BBQ is the current location of the "Big Indian" from Honest John's. *Author's collection.*

In 1970, Frank and Edna Pratt bought the restaurant, and their specialty quickly became fried chicken dinners. Locals loved to take their out-of-town guests to Pratt's Barn to share the southern hospitality. The Pratts quickly handed over the daily operations to their son, Tom, who was married to Chris Barger Pratt, daughter of Pal Barger.

Pratt's Barbeque is now the most popular catering business in the area. In 1979, the restaurant began offering this service, and it also helps plan parties and weddings.

RIVERVIEW CAFÉ

SURGOINSVILLE, TENNESSEE

The Golden Burger was opened in Surgoinsville as a sister restaurant to Golden Dairy in Rogersville. I have been told that the two restaurants were similar. Elizabeth DiBenedetto Woolridge reviewed the Golden Dairy on Facebook on November 19, 2016, saying, "If you are looking for ambience, go somewhere else. If you want good, freshly made comfort food, this is it." The Golden Dairy opened in 1970 and is still in business today, but the Golden Burger closed many years ago.

After the Golden Burger closed, Goldie Noe Woods opened Goldie's at the Surgoinsville location, but by the late 1980s to early 1990s, the building was open again under another name, Riverview Café.

The Williams' Store in Surgoinsville was owned by John. K. Williams. His daughter, Margaret, ran the store after his death. *Author's collection.*

The Riverview Café was a wonderful place to get an ice cream on a sweltering summer day. *Author's collection.*

Burgers and ice cream were the specialties of the Riverview Café, and locals remember sharing a cone with their grandparents after school or on a sweltering summer day. Those locals remember walking through town to the restaurant and passing the old Williams' Store run by John K. Williams. After Williams's death, his daughter, Margaret, kept the store running. It was later a laundromat and a secondhand antique store. Jeff Johnson's store was across the street.

Also on this quaint street were Mary Williams' Drug Store with a lunch counter, Fat Sam's Café and Pearson Grocery—later Carson Manis Grocery—and Gene Bellamy Garage.

SAMMY'S APEX

Johnson City, Tennessee

A restaurant known by many names, Sammy's Apex—Sammy's Apex Barbecue and Apex Barbecue—was found at 604 West Market Street on the corner of Roan Street. Sammy Collins owned the Tennessee Treasure Hunters and shared with me that "it is a great landmark. Great burgers. Great fries and coldest beer on tap in town."

TASTY FREEZE (OR CREAM)

Weber City, Virginia

There is controversy as to whether this great little restaurant was called Tasty Freeze or Tasty Cream, but either way, its special was hot fudge milkshakes. Tasty was in Weber City near where Food City now sits at the junction of Highway 23 and Wadlow Gap. Vergie Roberts, mother of Brent and Andrea, ran the place owned by Paul Bright of Hiltons, Virginia. Dari-Delite was a similar restaurant in Kingsport.

Right: Sammy's Apex and Barbecue in Johnson City was popular among college students. *Author's collection.*

Below: Locals could stop in for a quick bite at Dari-Delite. *Courtesy Kingsport Archives.*

TEDDY'S

Nickelsville, Virginia

Head down the Nickelsville Highway from Gate City, and you will find this old mom-and-pop restaurant. Teddy's, at 11804 Nickelsville Highway (or VA-71), is adorned with a mural showing its famous food. Teddy's owners, Teddy and Trish Kilgore, have been in the restaurant business for many years, as they started their first restaurant when they were in their early twenties.

Their first restaurant opened on the site where they currently run Teddy's Restaurant, but when the building burned down, they moved to another location. Later, the owners of the current location built on the property, and the Kilgores moved back. Teddy's was born. But before they moved back, Custard Stand served the Nickelsville area from that spot. Susie Gilmer Stapleton told me through the Facebook group "Scott County Faces, Places, and Memories" that "Howard and Reba Elliott owned it. Their son now runs Campus Restaurant in Gate City. Howard's sister Katherine ran Custard Stand after they owned it….Best hamburgers anywhere. I worked for Katherine back in the day."

When Teddy's Restaurant opened in 1985, Teddy was working at Eastman Chemical Company. Since retirement, though, he has worked full time at the little restaurant with delicious food that has put them on the map. The owners shared that they have been featured in *International Food Magazine* for their burgers. They also have good home-cooked meals and specialty ice creams. It has become a local hangout for the youth of the area, as they appreciate the locally owned business and its contributions to the community.

As I sat in the restaurant enjoying my meal, I noticed that one wall featured photos of people from the community. Trish explained that they started that in recent years for Nickelsville Days, a local festival, and they just never took them down. She gave the reason of "too lazy to take it down" as a joke, but I'm sure she knows that this memory wall makes this cozy restaurant even more endearing to local patrons and those who are just passing through. Over the years, the owners added more photos to create what they now affectionally call their Wall of Fame.

There is a lit Coca-Cola sign that lists shakes and ice cream on the same wall as the pictures of the community. Other walls hold a world map, a black-and-white clock and two white boards that list some desserts and the special of the day. The sweet tea represents the southern tradition well, as it offers a fresh way to cool off from the hot sun.

Teddy's diner in Nickelsville is a hidden treasure. *Author's collection.*

High school sports are an important part of small towns in the Appalachian Mountains, and it is no different in the tiny town of Nickelsville. There is a shrine-type area on one wall dedicated to the 1993 state champions in basketball. When Twin Springs High School students secured the championship, the locals took to the streets to celebrate. There was a family in a van visiting the area, and they were afraid when this happened because they didn't know about the championship—they just saw a mob of people heading toward their van. Once they saw they were not in danger, they continued with their visit of this small town nestled in Southwest Virginia.

Soft music plays in the background on an old dial radio perched on a corner shelf above the booths. Casual attire is expected. The red-and-white checkered plastic tablecloths give the whole room an atmosphere of a home-cooking restaurant.

It even offers free wi-fi to the patrons. Generous portions of fries and vegetables make this well worth the money—and you can eat here for about the same amount of money that you can get a meal at any of the local fast-food joints. If you would rather visit in the morning, biscuits and gravy or country ham seem to be the favorites.

Teddy and Trish never had children of their own, but their teenaged employees are like family. They watch these young workers grow up to be

Teddy's diner with beautiful artwork by Kathy Blair. *Author's collection.*

adults and start their own lives. Trish shared with me that many of her current employees were either children or grandchildren of their first employees from the mid-1980s. This is truly a family restaurant that gains more members as more employees are added.

If more of us valued food and cheer and song above hoarded gold,
it would be a merrier world.
—J.R.R. Tolkien

III

Night Life and Grills

Fame itself…doesn't really afford you anything more than a good seat in a restaurant.
—David Bowie

BUSY BEE RESTAURANT

KINGSPORT, TENNESSEE

One of the very first restaurateurs in the Kingsport area was Nick Karamblockis. He and his family were dedicated to the area even though his journey started far away. He was the owner and operator of Busy Bee Restaurant.

Nick Karamblockis was born in Greece and came to America in 1916. He married Leona Williams and they had two children in the Kingsport area: Mrs. Jack Ladd and Jim Karamblockis. During World War II, Karanblockis was fearful for the safety of his family in Greece. He yearned for news of his son. The Busy Bee owner finally received a letter on December 7, 1943, from his cousin in Chios, Greece. The Red Cross delivered the letter that had been mailed on February 23, 1943. With this letter, Karamblockis learned that "his son, Demetri, [was] safe in Athens, and that his mother and his brother's children [were] also well." The letter had been "investigated by the Board of Inquiry before" being delivered to Karamblockis.[22]

Karamblockis opened Busy Bee Lunch and was contracted to supply the meals for the local jail. He also gave free meals to members of the Kingsport City Police Force.[23]

CAVALIER GRILL

Gate City, Virginia

In the mid-1940s, Woody Duncan opened the Cavalier Grill, and it was open all night "for the convenience of the public." In 1944, there was a dance at the club with Fats Perry and His Orchestra. It offered a "refreshing atmosphere" to "meet your friends at the Cavalier." The location of the Cavalier changed through the years, and at one time, it was close enough to the Little Moccasin Creek to feel the ill effects of the creek flooding. No matter their location, the Cavalier was often under the watchful eye of law enforcement. It was often in trouble for illegal sale of alcohol and pinball machines used for gambling.

One night, from the parking lot of the Cavalier Grill, patrons reported seeing bright green round lights speeding across the black sky.

Woody Duncan owned the Cavalier Grill at two separate times. He opened the grill, and in 1961, there were reports that he was once again the owner. According to a death notice, Audrey Pendleton, owner of Pendleton's Restaurant, owned the Cavalier at one point. In 1991, there was a notice in the *Kingsport Times-News* stating that Carol Ann Gilbert, owner of the Cavalier Grill, had applied for an ABC license. The ABC in Virginia stands for the Alcohol Beverage Control Board, and Gilbert was applying for the right to sell beer in her establishment.

Woody Duncan also opened the Cavalier Grill No. 2 on Bristol Highway in the former E and W Barbeque building. Unfortunately, arson was committed at the No. 2 restaurant in 1949. Kingsport Fire Department responded to the call.

A note on some of the night life through the years: in the early 1980s, the police were watching many of the local establishments. Illegal alcohol sales and gambling were rampant throughout the town. There were many confiscations. On Sunday, October 16, 1983, the *Kingsport Times-News* reported confiscations. Although there was no mention of what was taken from which restaurants and stores, the paper did list those that were searched.

They were Overbrook Market, the Line, Brown Derby Grill, the Dutch Boy Drive-In No. 2, the Other Place (now Cavalier Grill), the Flamingo, the Liberty Café, Taylor's Grocery and Duffield Pool and Video.[24]

CLUB 81

KINGSPORT, TENNESSEE

I first read about Club 81 when researching the origins of Long Island iced tea. It was a members-only club that was portrayed by J.S. Moore, self-proclaimed storyteller rather than author, who writes on the area as a "rough and tumble underground dive by the bridge on Hwy. 81." There were signs everywhere saying, "Trespassers will be shot on sight" to warn away those who might interfere with business, including cops.[25]

The grand opening for Club 81 was May 19, 1948,[26] and a notice in the *Times-News* on May 12 noted the newly chartered club was a private, membership-only establishment. This was the "first dine and dance club in the Kingsport area in several years," but the "manager, Ike Valentine, had many years of experience."[27] Valentine hoped to build up to a variety in entertainment. He began with Sammy DeVault and his orchestra for dancing and planned to add floor shows and more bands for the six nights per week that the club was open.[28]

PEGGY ANN RESTAURANT AND COFFEE SHOP

KINGSPORT, TENNESSEE

In the *Kingsport Times-News* on December 23, 1970, it was reported,

> *Business of the week...Peggy Ann Restaurant...1459 E. Center Street... Phone 245-5512....We invite you to join with friends and family for an excellent meal in our relaxed surroundings. The delicious food is cooked to perfection and the service is excellent. Make it a habit to eat here often... we've many wonderful dishes for your feasting...all at reasonable prices. Our menu has something to suit every age and taste. See us for your parties,*

catering and carry-out. We're open 24 hours every day. Our business is your pleasure...may we serve you?

A.Y. Singleton and Paul Hopkins, Co-Owners, invite you and your family to dine with them often...for the best meal since you left home!

The Peggy Ann Restaurant was a wonderful place for parties. It offered catering and carry-out options too. The Peggy Ann Restaurant was open twenty-four hours per day and was considered the place to go after a late night out with friends or even after a long day at work. It was loved by most, and its closure saddened many. A.Y. Singleton died on November 22, 1977.

PHOENIX RESTAURANT AND GRILL

Kingsport, Tennessee

Five Points was known as the Greasy Corner, according to an editorial by Margaret N. Wimberly. She said, unfortunately, there were also areas of the town nicknamed Dirty Dozen, Cinch Row and Slab Town.[29]

The Phoenix Restaurant and Grill opened on May 31, 1939, in the same location as the former New Deal Restaurant. The Five Points location served many restaurants through the years and, in the 1980s, was the location of the Nickelodeon Pub.

In 1941, owners George Mitchell and Phillip Dimos sold beer to at least three minors at the Phoenix Restaurant and Grill, causing the owners to pay a twenty-five-dollar fine.[30] In 1942, Inspector J.F. King from the Department of Conservation, Division of Hotel and Restaurants, brought charges on three Kingsport restaurants, including the Phoenix Restaurant and Grill. Magistrate W.N. Showalter imposed a twenty-five-dollar fine plus costs to each of the three, which also included the Mayflower Restaurant and Southern Café. The charges stemmed from "improper sanitation of eating and drinking utensils and failure to require employs to furnish health cards before being employed." Three other restaurants were fined ten dollars each for violating the health card rule.[31]

According to an advertisement in the *Kingsport Times* on August 16, 1944, Phoenix Restaurant and Grill closed to implement improvements in equipment and decorations. It reopened on October 6. On its reopening, the Phoenix's owners donated all proceeds from the first day back in business to the National War Fund Relief. The owners also invited servicemen and women to enjoy a free meal when Greece was finally liberated.[32]

Phoenix Restaurant was sold to two well-known restaurant men. Charles W. Joseph had been affiliated with Charles Restaurant and Liberty Restaurant. Sam H. Massoud was a veteran of both World Wars. Both had several years in the restaurant business.[33]

In reference to Japan's surrender in 1945, Charles Joseph said, "This is the happiest day of our lives—I'll be glad to see all the boys back. This is the hour we've been waiting for and it should have come a year ago," Bill Thomason, a local resident, was pleased with the outcome, voicing that his only regret was that President Roosevelt wasn't alive to see it. Leon Fain, a cook at the Phoenix Restaurant and Grill, commented that the news would "make millions of mothers happy!"[34]

Charles Joseph and Sam Massoud remodeled the Phoenix Restaurant and Grill, giving credit for their success to their customers' loyalty.

In 1952, an article in the *Kingsport Times* spoke of the two oldest restaurant owners in Kingsport: Nick Karamblockis and Charles Joseph. Joseph was born in Lebanon, came to America in 1914 and settled in Kingsport in 1917. Charles Joseph was part owner of the Liberty Café in 1927 with Mike Kabool. He opened Charles Restaurant in 1941 and bought the Phoenix in 1945. He married Dorothy Hall Joseph, and they had three children, Charles W. Joseph Jr., Edward Joseph and Shirley Jean. Mr. Joseph Jr. spent some time in the navy before joining the air force, where he flew F-84 Thunder jets. By 1954, Edward Joseph had joined his father in running Phoenix Restaurant. He married Carol Yvonne French from Longview, Texas, and they both attended East Tennessee State.[35]

In 1976, Phoenix Restaurant owner and Knoxville resident George Mitchell was ordered to pay back taxes and fees of $16,000, $3,000 of which was from penalties and interests. He had not paid taxes in more than twenty years because, according to Mitchell, he misunderstood Kingsport tax laws since he was from another country. He thought that he didn't owe taxes on property that was not making any money. George Mitchell was given ninety days to pay or lose his property for good. At this point, the city had already taken possession of the property, and Mitchell was unable to regain possession, as he did not have the funds to pay the money owed to the city.

In 1933, owner J.W. Boulton sought a partner for his thriving business, the Rock House and Grill. *Author's collection.*

The Garden Grill operated in the Lynn Garden community of Kingsport. The building now houses Lynn Garden Restaurant. *Courtesy Kingsport Archives.*

THE ROCK HOUSE AND GRILL

Surgoinsville, Tennessee

In Surgoinsville, the Rock House Service Station and Grill was downtown near Riverview Café. It operated as a grill for many years but later became the Yankee Bee Car Repair and Alignment, the Tennessee Engine Rebuilder, Bait and Tackle fishing shop and a canoe rental business. I have reports of a Johnny Greer owning the property, but Everett and Joyce Greer actually owned the property. According to the Tennessee property data website, Herbert and Ruby Allen III now own the property with Michael and Patsy Allen.[36]

WOODY'S FLAMINGO GRILL

Gate City, Virginia

Woody's Flamingo Grill said that it was all about the beef. Its specialties were "deli sandwiches for lunch; steaks for dinner; no dessert available."[37] The anonymous reviewer in the *Kingsport Times-News* on March 27, 1981, gave the grill three and a half out of five stars. He went on to say that the service was "friendly, complete, and slow." When you entered Woody's Flamingo Grill, the restaurant was on the left and the bar was on the right, according to the review. But, the writer said, the bar had a small choice of name brand wines, and if you wanted something else, you would have to bring it in a brown bag for yourself.

My first memory in life is grilling my thumb to the griddle
in our restaurant in Cape Cod.
—Rachael Ray

IV

Drugstores

I am the kind of person who really will drive hours for a bowl of chili. I'm not a three-star restaurant kind of person; I'm just a food person.
—Nora Ephron

BROADWATER DRUG STORE

GATE CITY, VIRGINIA

B.J. Broadwater owned and operated Broadwater Drug Store for decades. He successfully cared for the people of his community and loved each customer he served. I had my first contact with Broadwater Drug not as a customer but as a loafer. I lived in Mt. Carmel and had no prescriptions, so I had no reason to visit a drugstore on a regular basis. However, Broadwater Drug Store had a lunch counter that my friend Christy Flanary Smith would often visit because her mom was employed at the store. I went into the business a few times with her to check in with her mom, to borrow a dollar or to just say hi. Christy speaks very highly of Mr. Broadwater and his employees. She fondly remembers that she and J.C. "Phil" Phillips would tease each other through the years.

She recently told me, "Broadwater Drug in Gate City was my FAV place to eat. When B.J. sold it, they stopped it. Biggest mistake. I still crave the food." She went on to say, "And the hotdogs and cherry choke!" She reminisced that she "once gave BJ a crybaby [sour candy] and "he took it and then I found him leaning over the trash can heaving. He swore he'd never take another piece of candy from me." Marvin Smith told me that

Broadwater Drugs in Gate City operated its lunch counter into the 1990s. *Courtesy Broadwater Drugs.*

B.J. Broadwater, owner and pharmacist, and J.C. "Phil" Phillips, pharmacist, posing at the counter at Broadwater Drugs in Gate City. *Courtesy Broadwater Drugs.*

the large cheeseburger was his choice and Virginia Gardner shared that she would drive from Johnson City for the burgers.

Mr. Broadwater sold his business, and it is now a branch of Walgreens but continues to go by the name of Broadwater Drug, and it still serves the community that Mr. Broadwater loved.

I found an article from August 25, 1974, that covered a dilemma in Southwest Virginia.[38] Beginning on July 1, 1974, it was legal to sell wine in drugstores in Virginia, but Scott County still prohibited beer and wine sales with greater than 3.2 percent alcoholic content. Writer Gene McClelland talked with several local drugstore owners. B.J. Broadwater was vocal on the subject, saying:

> *I wouldn't stock it if it were legal in Scott County....I don't think the change in law affects Scott County at all, but I wouldn't keep it here if it were legal. In the first place, special legislation allowing drug stores to keep wine is discriminatory. If we could keep it the department stores ought to be allowed to stock it as well. There's a place for everything, and the ABC store is the place for alcoholic beverages here. I don't want any part of it. I could get a license to handle liquor if I wanted it, but I believe it belongs in the ABC store down the street. Let them keep it there, and I won't have the problems connected with keeping it.*

Another interested party to this dilemma was Doug Agee of Gate City Drug Store. His store was in business from 1927 to the mid-1980s. Agee said, "We had enough problems six or seven years ago with people straining and drinking rubbing alcohol and paregoric, and we don't need the problems stocking wine would produce."

Earl Perry of Perry's Drug Store weighed in on the subject as well, saying, "We're too close to the church to even consider selling any wines, let alone fortified wines. We don't have the space for it, and it would create too many problems. We don't want it."

THE CITY DRUG STORE

ROGERSVILLE, TENNESSEE

Ken Smith owned the City Drug Store and the Medical Center in downtown Rogersville near the courthouse. Stephen Hyder from the Facebook group

"You Might Be from Hawkins County If..." shared with me: "Every day after high school, we would all pile into Ralph Jennings' [mother's] car [while she worked]. [Jennings] would take us downtown and we would invade the City Drug and take all of their booths. The booths were lined up [and] down the center store between the fountain bar and the products and we all ordered hamburgers, cheese sandwiches, chili...and milkshakes for our afternoon soiree and I went to work across the street at Hale's Music Studio."

CORNER DRUG STORE

ROGERSVILLE, TENNESSEE

On June 1, 1939, Corner Drug Store opened on the corner of Main and Church Streets in Rogersville with a "new modern soda fountain."[39] The president of Corner Drug Store was Mr. N.G. Mock. Mr. G.W. Bryan was vice president, and John Doty was secretary treasurer. The pharmacists promised the community that they would not use "cut-rate drugs" to increase their profits as some drugstores were doing at the time. They went on to say that they would not jeopardize their integrity for profits.[40] The Corner Drug Store was still in business in December 1964 because there was a mention in the *Rogersville Review* on Thursday, December 24, wishing everyone "Happy Holidays."

In the Thursday, September 15, 1960 edition of *Rogersville Review*, an article about White Store, which was a local grocery store, talked about how the store would be expanding. The new grocery would be self-service. There was a mention that the White Store had first opened in 1935 in the building where Corner Drug Store eventually opened in 1939.

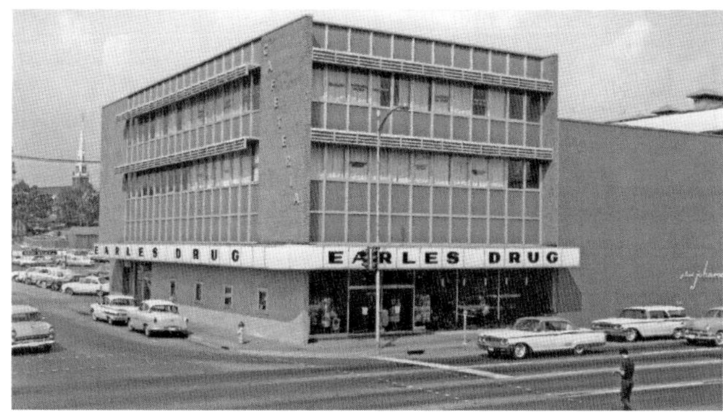

Earl's Drugs in downtown Kingsport. *Courtesy Kingsport Archives.*

HILBERT'S DRUG STORE

Jonesborough, Tennessee

A building owned by A.P. Shipley housed the Jonesborough drugstore. Fred T. Hilbert owned and operated the pharmacy from 1936 to 1969. Hilbert died in May 1972. A fire ravaged the drugstore on January 8, 1952, but "most of the damage came from the water to put the fire out."[41]

The location became Mauk's Jonesborough Pharmacy in late 1969.

SURGOINSVILLE DRUG

Surgoinsville, Tennessee

In 1965, Surgoinsville Drug shared a parking lot with Dr. Conner Lyons's parking lot a half block west of Highway 11W in Surgoinsville. There has continuously been a drugstore to serve the Surgoinsville community of Hawkins County since that time—until 2009 that is. At that time, CVS

Surgoinsville Pharmacy offers a hot lunch to patrons in the area. *Author's collection.*

The Surgoinsville Pharmacy has changed names and owners several times through the years, but it has always been a trusted source of quality medications and tasty food. *Author's collection.*

Pharmacy bought the older building and property in anticipation of opening a branch. John K. Williams was the former owner. However, CVS decided not to open a branch in Surgoinsville.

Currently, Beth Bryan owns Surgoinsville Pharmacy. She bought the business in 2012 and opened her Surgoinsville Pharmacy in the newer building next to the older one. Locals stop in for a bite to eat and to get their prescriptions. Bryan also has many gift items and cards for purchase in her cozy building.

The best fame is a writer's fame. It's enough to get a table at a good restaurant, but not enough to get you interrupted when you eat.
—Fran Lebowitz

V

Upscale and More

One cannot think well, love well, sleep well, if one has not dined well.
—Virginia Woolf

CIATTI'S ITALIAN GRILL

KINGSPORT, TENNESSEE

Ciatti's is another restaurant in Kingsport that is now missed. A chain restaurant based in Edina, Minnesota, Ciatti's felt more like a local treasure. It was donned in stylish décor that made the ambiance welcoming and led to an enjoyable time with family and friends. This was also a place where families could get a satisfying meal for a reasonable price. Appetizers were common ones, like mozzarella sticks and deep-fried ravioli. The main dish was sure to please, with seafood cannelloni, spaghetti, pasta primavera or tortellini to choose from and prices between four and nine dollars per plate.

In 1994, the *Star Tribune* in Minneapolis reported that Ciatti's Inc. was going to operate under a franchise agreement with Bruegger's Corp., so "Ciatti's will invest up to $7.5 million in bagel bakeries throughout the Dallas–Fort Worth market of Texas." It went on to say that Phil Danforth, president of Ciatti's Inc., was encouraged about the merger and said, "We see this as an opportunity to strengthen our company." Ciatti's was looking

Left: If you want pizza in Kingsport, Italian Village in the Fort Henry Mall is the place to go. *Author's collection.*

Right: Piccadilly Cafeteria has been in the Fort Henry Mall since the early '80s. *Author's collection.*

for ways to bolster profits and thought that selling bagels was the way to do so. It lost money in its 1993 fiscal year but gained in 1994—but not enough to win back all of the losses. However, just two years later, Ciatti's sued Bruegger's Bagel Bakeries over disputes on fundraising for new stores. Then in 1997, that same paper reported that Phillip Danforth said the corporation was "trying to grow the company."

Another great Italian restaurant in the Tri-Cities is the Fort Henry Mall staple Italian Village, which has served excellent food since the 1980s. Also in the mall is a cafeteria-style restaurant named Piccadilly. The restaurant looks and feels like a fancy stop in an upscale neighborhood.

DOGWOOD LANE

Jonesborough, Tennessee

David A. Phillips and Jeff Dupre owned Dogwood Lane at 109 Courthouse Square. The couple moved to the area from Miami, Florida, in 1981. At that time, there was no place in the Tri-Cities area where a person could sit down at a restaurant and have a drink unless it was a private club serving its members. Augistonos in Greeneville, Tennessee, was allowed to serve. With a one-dollar fee to join, Davy Crockett Ski Club could serve drinks. Pierless in Johnson City had a private club that could serve alcohol to its patrons. Owners Phillips and Dupre shared with me via a phone conversation that there were stores with drive-through windows where you could buy alcohol to take on your way. There was no way to stop a person from buying that alcohol and drinking it while driving. However, they were dismayed at the fact that their patrons could not come into their upscale restaurant and have a glass of wine with their meal. They tried to change this policy, and it did eventually change, but by that time, many of the restaurant owners who had fought for the change had moved on to other ventures.

DOWNTOWNER MOTOR LODGE

Kingsport, Tennessee

Once considered to be an upscale hotel and restaurant, the Downtowner Motor Lodge saw many changes throughout its tenure in downtown Kingsport. By the late 1980s, it had become a shell of itself and was eventually torn down to make room for other ventures in the area.

The Downtowner Motor Lodge as it stood in its prime. The downtown Kingsport location had several names and was also a restaurant. *Courtesy Kingsport Archives.*

KINGSPORT INN

Kingsport, Tennessee

The Kingsport Inn was quite the hotel and restaurant, and people still talk about its grandeur. When it opened in May 1917, locals and travelers alike were impressed by its majesty. A salesman traveling through Kingsport on May 17, 1917, J.H. Morris, said that the inn was the most "comfortable up-to-date hotel" he had ever stayed in during his twenty years of travel, as reported by the *Kingsport Times-News*. According to that same paper, Mrs. J.H. Mohar ran the beautiful hotel on the corner of Broad Street and Sullivan Street opposite the present-day Kingsport Public Library. The hotel was "artistically arranged," and it was beautifully designed, including the rooms, dining area and landscaping that surrounded the inn. The beauty welcomed weary travelers to feel at home for the night.

The 1920s brought about many changes for the Kingsport Inn. First, there was new construction to help the building and the business grow. Variable weather slowed construction, but it continued steadily. The new additions to the inn were estimated to cost in the range of $150,000. The Wurster Construction Company began work in March 1920. The additions to the Kingsport Inn doubled the capacity, with two stories and forty-four rooms, a writing room, a larger kitchen on the first floor and a larger dining room. This change helped form the inn as the patrons of later years loved it.

Later that year, Mr. Gasser of New York City became manager of the inn, but in December, after only three months, Mr. Gasser retired to his home in New York City. At that time, H.C. Burden took control of managing responsibilities. Burden had experience, as he was a "hotel man" from Tate Springs, Tennessee. Burden's assistants, J.C. Tipton and J.M. Byrd, helped run the inn.

The *Times-News* reported on December 10, 1920, "Mr. Burden is a hotel man of extensive experience, and it is believed he will keep the reputation of the Inn at its high standard of the past," and his "family will join him here in ten days or so."

Throughout its many years of service to the community, the Kingsport Inn hosted several events. Local groups and clubs often met at the inn, and it hosted social events like afternoon teas, luncheons and banquets.

As much as the Kingsport Inn was loved, all good things must end. The *Kingsport Times-News* reported on April 5, 1960, "For Sentimental reasons.... You should buy some part of Kingsport Inn....A famous landmark of Kingsport, Tenn....The Building and all Furniture, furnishings, and equipment WILL BE SOLD!...The Sale Will Start Tuesday Morning, April 5th [at] 9 A.M. and will continue each weekday from 9 O'clock in the Morning until 9 P.M." The ad then went on to tell how to go about buying these items, including the china from the kitchen.

The building was to be sold as is or by breaking the building into parts. Bowers Bros. Selling Agents and Auctioneers and Red Wheel Auction Company handled the sale of the property. In the case that the building and its contents were not sold on time, there was to be a public auction on Friday, April 15, at 10:00 a.m. Among the people who remember the inn, there is much speculation as to why it closed in the way it did, but the truth seems to lie in the upkeep—or rather the lack of the upkeep—of the building itself. As the building fell into disarray, the owners felt the only recourse would be to close the inn and dismantle the building brick by brick. Susan Claytor said that her neighbors at that time "built most of their house with bricks from" the Kingsport Inn.

I had a discussion with several other people about the Kingsport Inn on the Facebook group "You Know You Grew Up in Kingsport If..." Barbara Sanders talked about how beautiful the building was and questioned why it had been torn down. Having seen pictures of the restaurant in its heyday, I wondered, too.

David Sizemore said, "It was in terrible structural condition...and then the health dept. shut down its kitchen." After that, the owners had no choice but to close the business, as the remodel would have been too costly.

Steve Howard said that he had heard that the building was falling "into disrepair, even while being used."

Allison Looney Coven said that her mother was lucky enough to have been given "a couple of chairs" that Allison now owns. She added that the Kingsport Inn "was a beautiful 'Old South' Inn!"

And Robert Dean said that he had "read several years ago...that Bette Davis and her family stayed there once when they were driving through the area."

OLDE WEST DINNER THEATER

Johnson City, Tennessee

The Olde West Dinner Theater opened in the 1960s and was the place to celebrate anniversaries and engagements or to have a leisurely night out with the family. Local schools introduced students to the fine art of theater during morning school performances. That was my first taste of theater. In kindergarten at Mt. Carmel Elementary School, my first field trip was to Olde West Dinner Theater. It was a morning performance. I do not remember much about the particular play, but I do remember the glamour of it all—the stage, actors, costumes, lights—it was all so beautiful. The students sat on the floor around the stage. I sat in the front row with my best friend, Tammy Aistrop, and we held hands as we watched the actors move across the stage.

The Olde West Dinner Theater opened in October 1966 on Airport Road (now Highway 75) in what is now Johnson City. The restaurant ran for several years but closed in the late 1980s or early 1990s. In the mid-1990s, a couple bought the dinner theater and created a medieval theme. They rebuilt the outside to look like a castle, and the performances were stories from medieval times. Unfortunately, this venture did not last long, and the restaurant sat empty again. Now, the building is gone, and there are storage units on the property.

ORANGE BOWL RESTAURANT

Rogersville, Tennessee

The Orange Bowl Restaurant was in business in Rogersville for a long time. It was across the street from what was then K-Mart. Matt Kenner told me, "My grandfather used to take me to the Orange Bowl as a child. I was able to go once as a teenager before it closed. The food may not have [been] the best, but the memories last forever." He went on to tell me that the restaurant closed and was torn down in the 1990s.

THE PARSON'S TABLE

JONESBOROUGH, TENNESSEE

As told by the Parson's Table owner Jimmy Neil Smith:

> *My grandmother cooked in several Jonesborough restaurants during the 1950s. She was well known for her cream pies. When I was a young boy, I would spend the weekend with her and my grandfather. So, when she would go to work, I would go to the restaurant with her. I sat in the back of the kitchen and watched my grandmother work. I became enamored with restaurants, and even when I was sixteen years old, I realized I wanted to own and operate a restaurant in my hometown of Jonesborough.*
>
> *Then, in early 1973, when I was twenty-five, I scraped together $10,000, partnered with my mother and secured a loan from the Small Business Administration. We bought the old First Christian Church, found just above the railroad tracks in downtown Jonesborough. It was there, in that century-old, abandoned church, that we would open our restaurant—the Parson's Table.*
>
> *The old church, when first used in 1874, was considered an "ornament to the town" and a "magnificent temple." But money problems plagued the church membership, the church was eventually closed and the congregation merged with another church in downtown Jonesborough. When my mother and I bought the building, the old church was a woodworking shop.*
>
> *After a full restoration, the church became the Parson's Table. When the restaurant opened, we served both lunch and dinner, and our menu offered a wide variety of entrees—from hamburgers to steaks to chicken and dumplings. We tried to attract both the lunch and dinner markets in Jonesborough. But within a few months, we realized we were failing. It quickly became obvious. We were trying to be all things to all people, and the quality of the food we served was mediocre at best.*
>
> *So, to begin to overcome the failures, we made some personnel changes, and I left my teaching job at Science Hill High School in Johnson City to give full attention to the restaurant's operation. During the first months of 1974, the Parson's Table was transformed. The menu was stripped down to only five entrees, and all of the other food items—the Parson's Brew and peanuts, fresh relishes, vegetable soup and flat bread, green beans, stewed apples, sweet potato pudding, homemade bread, a drink, and, finally, hot apple fritters for dessert—came with the entree. The five*

Left: The Parson's Table as patrons leave the front of the restaurant. *Courtesy of the Jonesborough/Washington County History Museum and Archives, a department of the Heritage Alliance, Jonesborough, Tennessee.*

Right: Jimmy Neil Smith, owner of the Parson's Table, standing in front of his popular restaurant. *Courtesy of the Jonesborough/Washington County History Museum and Archives, a department of the Heritage Alliance, Jonesborough, Tennessee.*

entrees included country ham, chicken and dumplings, baked stuff[ed] *pork chop, catfish and pot roast of beef.*

During the following months, the Parson's Table gradually overcame its early failures, and the number of diners began to grow. Soon, the eighty-plus seats in the old church could no longer accommodate the growing level of business during the weekends. But while our diners enjoyed our five entrees, we were told that there was something missing: steak.

So, to increase our seating ability and to offer a variety of steaks that many diners desired, we transformed the church parsonage, found at once behind the church, into the Widow Brown's. The two restaurants had separate entrances but shared a kitchen and other back-of-the-house operations.

Following the successful model of the Parson's Table, the Widow Brown's offered a very limited number of entrees, and all of the other food items—honey-dipped chicken legs, pickled beets and peaches, slaw,

The Parson's Table sign that is still decorated for the seasons, though the restaurant has not been open for a few years. *Author's collection.*

bowl of salad, a rosin-baked potato, homemade bread, a drink and an assortment of desserts. Entrées included a choice of steaks and ribs, chicken, and trout. And all of the entrees were grilled over real, charred wood, and the baked potatoes were cooked in a kettle of rosin—all in a glassed gazebo beside the parsonage where the diners could watch the food being prepared.

Once again, the concept, now used in both the Parson's Table and Widow Brown's, proved successful, and the new restaurant began attracting its own growing following of diners. For twelve years, the Parson's Table and Widow Brown's were successful and well-respected restaurants in the northeast corner of Tennessee. But then, something happened that would change all of that.

In the early to mid-1980s, Johnson City and Kingsport approved the service of mixed beverages in the cities' restaurants, and new restaurants popped up everywhere. But, at that time, Jonesborough prohibited the sale of mixed beverages. Having a glass of wine or a cocktail with dinner was very appealing, and many of the diners at the Parson's Table and Widow Brown's began trying the new restaurants. The number of diners at the two Jonesborough restaurants dropped by two-thirds. And despite some major changes in our operation to lower costs, we were not able to financially overcome the two-thirds drop in business. So, the Parson's Table and Widow Brown's closed.

Within a year, however, Jeff and Debra Myron purchased the restaurant, continued its operation as the Parson's Table, but they featured an upscale, classical menu. The Widow Brown's continued to remain closed. For twelve years, the Parson's Table continued to find success. But today, the church and the parsonage sit unused, and an iconic restaurant in northeast Tennessee is closed.

David Joe Miller told me in an email message on June 24, 2019, that each restaurant had "excellent food and service and a reputation known for hundreds of miles. First time I ever had a pine rosin baked potato. Billy Bledsoe, the Jonesborough artist was a cook there. My great-aunt Pearl, sister-in-law of Ola Rush of Rush's restaurant used to make all the pies for the restaurant."

SKOBY'S AND SKOBY'S WORLD

KINGSPORT, TENNESSEE

Fred and Helen Barger opened Skoby's in 1946, and it was the high-class restaurant of the Tri-Cities throughout its tenure. Kingsport was lucky to have such a treasure for as long as it did. Fred succeeded in everything he did, with a career in the restaurant business and, before that, lettering in several sports in high school.

Skoby's restaurant had a beautiful outdoor structure and was eloquently decorated. Themed rooms donned antiques—both in decorations and in furniture. Fred Barger Sr. died in 1971, and his son, Fred "Pal" Barger Jr., took over operations of the restaurant that then became Skoby's World. Neither the quality of food nor the fantastic prices took a nosedive, but there were some changes in how things were run. On Bob Lawrence's Kingsport blog, John Osborne describes that when Pal took over operations, Skoby's World "offered a department store of dining"[42] with themed rooms like the Orient and the Galley. Helen Barger survived her husband by eight years and left everything to Pal.

Alan Howell of Dixie Barbecue got his start at Skoby's. That's where he learned his love of food and the restaurant business. He worked for Pal Barger and admits that he learned everything he knows about the food industry while working there. He worked in every position available, including manager, during his years with Skoby's World. Pal ran Pal's Sudden Service while running Skoby's, and Howell told me that Skoby's World did not make great profits, so Pal supplemented Skoby's World's needs with profits from Pal's Sudden Service. It was not that Skoby's World did not have the ability to make money, but Pal refused to charge the prices that would make great profits in this landmark restaurant. With caviar on the salad bar, you can only imagine what a restaurant like this would have charged in a major city, but

Pal Barger made sure that the people of northeast Tennessee and Southwest Virginia could afford the luxuries.

David Joe Miller told me that he would call ahead when making reservations for dates to have roses waiting for his lucky companion.

Skoby's closed in 2005. Kimball Sterling, an auctioneer who specializes in antique and unique sales, auctioned the antique collection from the restaurant. They auctioned the furniture as well as menus and other memorabilia. The public moved in quick for the sale, and many people took home items they would cherish forever.[43]

At this time, Pal Barger donated the restaurant to Virginia Intermont College for its culinary arts department. In 2010, the college disbanded its operations at the restaurant, and the former glory was demolished. The school closed for good in 2014 after losing accreditation.

TRAYER'S

Kingsport, Tennessee, and Bristol, Virginia/Tennessee

Jack Trayer, owner of several restaurants in the area, began his successful career by buying a barbecue stand on Moore Street in Bristol, Virginia, with an older Ed Anderson. Trayer and Anderson met in Staunton, Virginia, where Trayer had attended Dunsmore Business College. After graduating, he took a job in West Virginia but then went back to Staunton to run a business with Anderson. They soon sold and moved to the Tri-Cities, where they happened on the chance to buy the Red, White, and Blue Barbecue. During the Depression, Anderson ran the barbecue stand while Trayer took a job in New York City so that he could take night classes for business administration at Columbia University. On his return to Bristol the next year, he met and then married Dorothy Cigrand, who was from Chicago but was living in Bristol while attending Virginia Intermont College.

When Anderson decided to retire in 1938, Jack and Dot Trayer bought his share of the barbecue stand and ran it until Trayer joined the U.S. Navy in 1944. It was on his return to Bristol some twenty months later that Trayer started to make a name for himself.

Jack and Dot Trayer bought a piece of land on Moore Street, and the first Trayer's Restaurant was born. This was the first downtown business to offer a parking area for its customers.

Soon afterward, the Trayers bought the lots sold at public auction from the former King's Mountain Memorial Hospital and erected Trayer's Too. They eventually bought the old Beacon Drive-In location in Kingsport and opened Trayer's Drive-In.

Trayer also owned three Holiday Inns in the area—one in Kingsport, one in Bristol and one in Johnson City. They also owned Business Services, a printing company in Bristol; Interstate Bowl; Bristol Buffet; Southside Delicatessen; Hotel Bristol; and Trayer's Food Shop, among other businesses in the Tri-Cities. Jack Trayer was also the president of the Virginia Restaurant Association for a time in the 1940s.

The Associated Press, as printed in the *Kingsport News* on November 20, 1952, reported, "Restaurateurs Elect Officer from Abingdon," which included Jack Trayer as a chosen director.

Then, the *Kingsport News* reported on February 20, 1954, that a "Tri-State Group Moves to Boost Area Promotion." The area included was North Carolina, Virginia and East Tennessee. Among the directors elected was Jack Trayer of Bristol.

Trayer was often found helping his community. He allowed his restaurants to be used as meeting places, and he supported the youth in the area. He even bought hogs from junior growers of the 4-H competitions.

Behind the Holiday Inn Hotel and Restaurant, you can see what was then a popular outdoor shopping mall that included a grocery store. Those buildings are now gone, and a Walmart has taken their places. *Courtesy Kingsport Archives.*

Trayer's seen here from Kingsport. *Courtesy Kingsport Archives.*

The Christmas holiday in 1952 had been great for businesses in the area, as people shopped more than normal. Several businesses in downtown Kingsport came to fruition, as there were shopping centers, motels and restaurants rising on the landscape and bringing a more modern look to the model city. One such business was the groundbreaking for the construction of "Holiday Inn Motel near the clover-leaf of Lynn Garden Drive and U.S. Highway 11-W." Jack Trayer held the franchise of this business, and he was a principal stockholder. It was planned to open in mid-April 1961. The motel also housed a nice restaurant, which was one of many that Trayer would run through the golden years.

The Trayers divorced in the mid 1960s, and Jack eventually remarried. Jack Trayer was admired by locals throughout his life. He died in 2006.

There is no love sincerer than the love of food.
—George Bernard Shaw

VI

Cafés and Restaurants

And the idea of just wandering off to a café with a notebook and writing and seeing where that takes me for awhile is just bliss.
—J.K. Rowling

ARCH FAIN'S CAFÉ

ROGERSVILLE, TENNESSEE

Arch Fain was a legend. He worked hard his entire life and made strides that put him on the map. In 1907, Fain went to work at Tate Springs Hotel in Grainger County, Tennessee. He was a combination kitchen boy, waiter and bellhop. He worked under the supervision of Captain Thomas P. Thompson. It was typical at the time to pay workers at the end of their tour, and Arch Fain was no different. He was paid thirty-five dollars for ninety days of work. It was three dollars a week, but he was fined one dollar for fighting. The head chef at Tate Springs Hotel was W.M. Watkins, who was one of the most outstanding African American chefs. Fain credited Watkins for his success.[44]

Arch was no stranger to kitchen work. In the late 1800s, Arch's father, James Fain, had a restaurant named James' Place. He had one room and a kitchen. There was only one door. A window in the back lit the kitchen. All water in the restaurant was from a cistern that sat in the back of the building. He used a step-stove, which burned $1.25 of wood every day. He paid $4.00

A popular bakery in downtown Kingsport in the mid-twentieth century. *Courtesy Kingsport Archives.*

per month for rent and had $12.00 per year for electric lights. People would walk for miles to eat at James Fain's café. He had only two tables—one sat six to eight people and the other ten to twelve. The restaurant was on Main Street in Rogersville and was a main stop for "river rafts men and the travelers from Bristol and Knoxville."[45]

Arch Fain quit school when he was twelve years old to become a miner in Osaka, Virginia, with his brother. Arch was a trapper, which meant that he opened and closed the mine section doors. His brother did not want him to be stuck in a mine for the rest of his life, so he forced Arch to quit in 1906 to find a better life.

From 1936 until 1946, Arch Fain was a chef on the Southern Railroad. He traveled through Roanoke, Atlanta, Washington, Mobile and Montgomery, but he did not like the "trainman's life."[46] One of Fain's biggest accomplishments came from his life on the train. He served as chef on several Roosevelt Specials when Franklin D. Roosevelt traveled across the South campaigning for president of the United States. This was a position that a chef was to be specifically assigned to, and Fain was chosen from more than sixty chefs to prepare the food. He was one of two chefs on the train; the other was Chef Bob Atkins from Atlanta, Georgia. Arch told friends that he once saw the president as he walked toward the diner. At another time,

FDR sent a message to Fain about his love of a special dish of fish that Fain had prepared for him. The fish had been sent to the president by Senator Joe T. Robinson of Arkansas. He sent two ten-pound black bass in the late 1930s. The presentation of the fish was as delectable as the taste. The plate on which the dish was served bore the seal of the United States.

Fain also worked at the Hotel Como in Hot Springs, Arkansas, on two separate occasions; the Goldman Hotel at Fort Smith, Arkansas, which he opened with other chefs in 1909; the Missouri Pacific in 1911, which is when he married Nora Brice; the Farragut Hotel in Knoxville; and Pressmen's Home, where he had the honor of cooking the food for International Printing Pressmen's Union Convention for several years. He also served on cruises on the Great Lakes, at the Republican National Committee and on Mackinac Island.

Arch Fain opened his own restaurant in Rogersville. There, he had the pleasure of serving U.S. senators Estes Kefauver (Tennessee), Albert Gore (Tennessee), Tom Connally (Texas) and Hattie Carraway (Arkansas), as well as U.S. Supreme Court justice Hugo Black, Governor Frank Clement and Representatives Carroll Reece and Pat Sutton.

Randolph Cupp told me, "My mother said it was THE PLACE back then. All the Senior Banquets for RHS [Rogersville High School] were held there." The restaurant was famous in the area and from quite a distance as well. Yes, Arch Fain was a legend in Hawkins County and beyond.

The Smoke House is just one of the many restaurants that have come and gone in Kingsport. *Courtesy Kingsport Archives.*

BEV'S RESTAURANT

Church Hill, Tennessee

George S. and Beverly J. Poe were the owners of Bev's Restaurant in the early 1980s. Amy Lindsey Justice told me that the restaurant "started out [in the] old Skeleton Motel in Church Hill, then moved to the [Church Hill] shopping center where Oakwood was." Justice worked there, and her daughter now owns Caddy's Corner in Kingsport.

BUSH AND WARD RESTAURANT

Gate City, Virginia

Bush's was on the main street in Gate City, Virginia, next to the Gate City Theatre. The owners, John W. Bush and L.D. Ward, made a good name for their restaurant during their tenure in Gate City. Unfortunately, a fire "destroyed the restaurant along with neighboring stores."[47]

BYRD'S RESTAURANT

Johnson City, Tennessee

Owners Harry Byrd and Faye Byrd opened Byrd's Restaurant, where "room service is the proud delivery service for the fantastic home cooking of the Byrd's Restaurant."[48]

Although at the time it was no laughing matter, a horrible smell once filled the restaurant. It was found that a skunk had taken residence under the restaurant. The fragrance of the skunk was shared throughout the restaurant, causing it to close until the animal could be persuaded to find another home.

Byrd's Restaurant's patrons came from all over, as travelers would seek it out because of its excellent reputation of quality, home-cooked meals. The restaurant and many of the surrounding businesses were bought and then all of these buildings were demolished in the name of a renewal project. The restaurant had been in business for sixteen years on December 23, 1972, and the last meal was served at 3:00 p.m.

CENTER STREET RESTAURANT

Kingsport, Tennessee

Center Street Restaurant was a staple in the Kingsport community. Located on the corner of West Center and Roller Streets, it was a handy place to stop for lunch or dinner. It was across the street from the Kingsport Press,

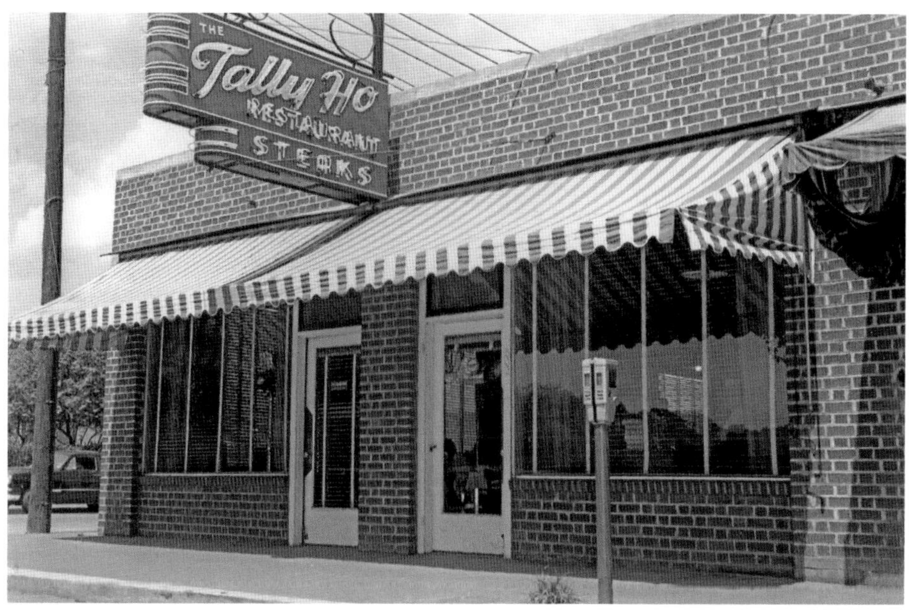

Tally-Ho was once an exotic local favorite. *Courtesy Kingsport Archives.*

Nick's Restaurant near the Fort Henry Mall in Kingsport. *Author's collection.*

a book binding factory in Kingsport, so the restaurant often hosted guests from the factory on their days or evenings off from work. Jack May opened the restaurant, and the Franciscos later bought the successful business from him. In 1957, Center Street Restaurant opened in the same building where the Center Street Grill had opened in 1947 and operated successfully for ten years.

Jack May's Center Street Restaurant offered homestyle food, including a hot roast beef sandwich served with mashed potatoes and brown gravy, and it had a lot of pies for dessert. Locals who remember the restaurant from May's days say that it was the best place to get a delicious meal in Kingsport.

The servers were dressed all in white—shoes and dresses—and they wore hair nets and a real smile, according to Janice Jones, who is a member of a local group of remembrance. Another member of this group, Skot DeSpain, commented that at Jack May's Center Street Restaurant, there was "great food and service. They made you feel special, important, respected."

Everyone loved the pies at Center Street Restaurant. They were made by a man named Harold, who was legally blind. He was a veteran and was shy, but some say that he made the most delicious pies around. For a time, Mary Bowling worked in the kitchen making rolls and the salads that everyone enjoyed.

When Jack May sold Center Street, he opened Jack's on Main Street in Kingsport, across from the foundry.

The lunch bar at Center Street Restaurant. *Author's collection.*

CHARLIE'S RESTAURANT

ROGERSVILLE, TENNESSEE

Although I could not find much information on Charlie's Restaurant in Rogersville, there were some comments about it in the Facebook group "You Might Be from Hawkins County If…" Qualls said that it had "the best chicken tenders and mashed potatoes."

"I loved the bbq plate and the salads," said Brittany Kay Hughes.

It was so good, in fact, that Wendy Hicks commented, "I just said last week…I'd kill for that chicken."

DANIEL BOONE TRAIL RESTAURANT

GATE CITY, VIRGINIA

Daniel Boone was an integral part of Gate City and Weber City becoming successful Southwest Virginia towns. So, the Daniel Boone Trail Restaurant was named to honor his contributions.

Bruce J. Riggs, a successful businessperson, owned Trail Restaurant. He also owned the Daniel Boone Trail Motel and the adjacent gas station at the intersection of Highway 58-42 West and Highway 23. The latter highway runs through the center of Weber City and offers a way to circumvent downtown Gate City.

DINNER BELL RESTAURANT

JONESBOROUGH, TENNESSEE

The Dinner Bell Restaurant was on West Main Street in Jonesborough. The restaurant offered "Old Fashioned Home Cooked Meals," according to an advertisement in the *Johnson City Press* on October 24, 1980. The Dinner Bell Restaurant was found behind the Chester Inn. In 1990, Charles Humpston bought the Dinner Bell and then opened the Family Tree Restaurant.[49]

Patrons having a laugh outside the Dinner Bell in Jonesborough. *Courtesy Chad Fred Bailey.*

Chester Inn Sandwich Shop in Jonesborough. *Courtesy of the Jonesborough/Washington Country History Museum and Archives, a department of the Heritage Alliance, Jonesborough, Tennessee.*

HARKLEROAD CAFÉ

Surgoinsville, Tennessee

Jacob Oscar Harkleroad attended and received a diploma from Surgoinsville High School. While a student, he and his classmates had to take their own water to school, as there was not a well on the location. Harkleroad and his friends would play jokes on one another by stealing and hiding these water jugs. In 1942, Harkleroad was one of many draftees leaving for service.

After service, Harkleroad opened a café in his hometown of Surgoinsville. The official name of the restaurant was Harkleroad Café, but most people—then and now—call the restaurant Fat Sam's. This was apparently his nickname. On the other hand, his family primarily called him Oscar.

The restaurant was found across the street from Williams' Store. The building is no longer there, but it sat next to the present-day Surgoinsville Police Department with Mary Williams' Drug Store.

"Fat Sam's" restaurant in Surgoinsville. *Courtesy of Johnny Greer.*

Harkleroad and his wife, Mary, lived on Church Street, and he worked at Tennessee Eastman Company in Kingsport. He was a member of Surgoinsville Baptist Church, Clay Lodge F&AM and was a Scottish Rite Mason.

In 1961, Oscar Harkleroad put his restaurant up for sale or rent, as he had other interests that he wanted to pursue. Mickey Houston told me that his parents ran the café in the early 1970s.

One of Harkleroad's interests was the new Hawkins County Municipal Airport. In 1965, the airport was a big deal for a small town. The runway was completed in June with 3,500 feet paved. The hangar would be completed that fall. On weekends, the community would gather at the airport to enjoy the company of others, creating a "carnival type atmosphere." Pilots would take passengers on rides, and Oscar Harkleroad would assist the passengers to the planes.[50]

Mary Matthews Harkleroad was my husband's aunt. According to the *News-Herald* in Port Clinton, Ohio, my father- and mother-in-law, William "Loyd" and Muriel Matthews, and their sons, Ricky and Ronnie, visited the Harkleroads' home in April 1970. They were traveling with J.D. Mowell and his son, Dennis. The family had been living in Port Clinton, Ohio, for work. Loyd was taking his mother, Lura, home, as she had been visiting in Ohio.

Oscar Harkleroad died in September 1970. Loyd and Muriel moved their family back to Tennessee in 1975.

JACK'S RESTAURANT

KINGSPORT, TENNESSEE, WEBER CITY AND CLINCHPORT, VIRGINIA

Through the years, there have been three Jack's Restaurants in the area. The first was found in downtown Kingsport. When Jack and Jeanette May sold the Center Street Restaurant, they decided that they were not ready to leave the restaurant business, so they opened Jack's Restaurant downtown. They offered many of the same items as they had in the past stores.

Second, Jack's Restaurant in Weber City, Virginia, was a favorite of mine in the 1970s. We had a few church lunches there, but my favorite time was when my grandmother Edla Haynes Strong was given an awards dinner and a plaque for a job well done. She was the Weber City clerk for much of her life, and she was the secretary/receptionist/bookkeeper for the Weber City Volunteer Fire Department. I do not remember which of these entities was

This Jack's Restaurant was found in Clinchport, Virginia. *Author's collection.*

Fresh fish can always be found at the Riverfront Café. *Author's collection.*

awarding her at this time, but I remember the smile on her face as she held that plaque at the head of the table. This Jack's specialty was the old-timey chicken and dumplings offered on Sundays. It also consistently offered a Friday fish fry.

Third, Jack's Restaurant in Clinchport, Virginia, was half a mile past the Clinch River Bridge, going north on Highway 23. It had home-cooked meals as well as great burgers and fries. The owners and their staff were always friendly and welcoming. The restaurant was divided into two rooms by a narrow doorway. If you sat in the back room, you could overlook the river as you ate. The restaurant also had an apartment downstairs that was sometimes used by the owners to get a quick start in the mornings but was often rented out to others.

Jan-Mar Restaurant

Kingsport, Tennessee

Jan-Mar was a popular diner for the working man as well as the elite, as Congressman Jimmy Quillen often ate there. *Author's collection.*

John and Mary Greene opened their restaurant in the early 1950s. It sat near the train station on Broad Street. Jan-Mar, the phonetic spelling of John Mary in French, became the name to know to dine with some of the more elite in the area. Jimmy Quillen is just one of the famous people who ate there often.

A modest restaurant with only a few booths and barstools, Jan-Mar was run by the couple until John's death in the early 1970s. That's when Mary realized her business capabilities. She stepped up and ran the business because she didn't have a choice, and in 1979, she decided to fight city hall over road closings that directly affected her business.

LIBERTY CAFÉ

KINGSPORT, BRISTOL AND ROGERSVILLE, TENNESSEE, AND GATE CITY, VIRGINIA

M.F. Kabool, A.M. Joseph and manager Feres Ackle opened Liberty Café's Kingsport location on August 18, 1927, in the Shaheen building at Five Points. Kabool and Ackle were from Iaeger, West Virginia, and Joseph was formerly associated with the Palace of Sweets, which had been in the same building as the new endeavor. N. Shaheen had apartments for rent above the café.

An ad claiming that Liberty Café was the best place in Kingsport to eat with the best service and the most delicious food ran in the *Kingsport Times* on February 26, 1928. The owners thanked the community, saying, "We made up our minds to locate a high class, up-to-date restaurant in Kingsport last year because we believed Kingsport to be a progressive, wide-awake city, with wonderful opportunities. Our confidence in the city has been justified. For the past year it has grown rapidly, and this fine growth is still continuing. We are proud to have cast our lot in such a progressive community, and to have become a part of the community."

Nestled on the corner of Cherokee and Sullivan Streets, Liberty Café was afforded the success of the other businesses there, and many have said it was a city in a city because there were so many successful establishments in a three-block radius of Five Points.

In 1929, an article in the *Kingsport Times-News* reported that Liberty Café was one of the best places in all of Kingsport to dine for visitors and locals alike. However, there are reports that in 1928, the Cherokee Creamery No. 2 moved into the same location, implying that Liberty Café closed after only one year. It was a second location of the local creamery, with its main location keeping its spot down the road at the corner of Cherokee and Market Streets. The difference was that No. 2 offered a deli and soda fountain along with the usual milk products.

Kabool, who was a Mason with the Knights Templar and a member of the American Legion, died on April 29, 1938, at the age of forty-two. Afterward, C.W. Joseph and Stellis Mallis Christy took over management of Liberty Café. This was during the Second World War. Christy knew about war from firsthand experience because he lived in a war zone before he moved to the United States, so when World War II began, he held a fear that most Kingsportians could not understand. "He spent much of the period of the first World War in Constantinople where soldiers of many nations fought fiercely for possession of that strategic city."[51]

Stellis Christy came to the United States after World War I, and he admitted that "he [was] glad to be in a country where air raids [were] a topic of conversation and not a grim reality."[52] He said:

> *Anyone who has never been in an air raid can't possibly realize what it is like….There's such a feeling of helplessness. The soldiers are kept busy and have little time to think; but the civilians, unable to offer any resistance to the attacks, can only flee and hide and suffer and wish they had some way to strike back….After a while, when you've seen your best friends and maybe your mother and brothers and sisters struck down all around you, you get so you don't care what happens….Then it's just a matter of endurance until the war is over and you can live again.*[53]

Liberty Café was locally famous as a pub-type establishment and had many colorful stories. Many are about a chef who was employed there for a time. Andy Turner was an African American Kingsportian who had the reputation of being one of the greatest chefs in the area, but he had his own problems. On October 9, 1926, Turner was jailed on a charge of drunkenness and driving a vehicle while intoxicated. Another time, Andy Turner and his female roommate were charged with possession of two gallons of moonshine whiskey. This was not unusual for the people of this town, but Andy Turner got caught. Then, the event that put him on the map left him missing part of himself. During the time that he was employed at Liberty Café, he was hit by a train on Long Island in Kingsport. He lost a finger in this August 1940 battle of man vs. machine but continued on otherwise with no problems.

In 1941, Pauline Masters from Fall Branch took over management of the Liberty Café. She had ten years of experience managing the Andrew Jackson Tavern and working at Knoxville's Master's Café. She also taught in a "government cooking school in Washington where boys were trained to become chefs." She learned much of her trade while attending East Tennessee State College (now East Tennessee State University). While Masters was there, Liberty Café was a National Restaurant Association member. The association had been formed in 1919 in Kansas after a successful boycott to lower the price of eggs, and it consistently set standards for the restaurant industry.

By 1945, Liberty Café was no longer in business, and Edward's Hardware took its place when it opened for business on December 1.[54] However, shortly thereafter, Liberty Café reopened in the same spot. Still going strong in January 1948, it was granted "restaurant and cigarette licenses" for the Sullivan Street address.[55] The restaurant again reopened in March 1948, with J.K. Joseph as owner, and one year later, Mr. and Mrs. C.H. Spencer became managers. Once again, one year later saw the reopening of the restaurant under the management of Ed Taylor and then again in May 1951 with N.M. Ollie and Charles Joseph.

There were other Liberty Cafés in the area—some related and some not. In Bristol, Liberty Café was viable for several years; however, in 1951, operator Farris M. Hassin died.

A Liberty Café was at street level on Jackson Street, in Gate City, with an inn offering rooms to travelers above. In 1949, Frank and Janie Harris visited the restaurant for their first date. Eighteen years later, they bought the inn, refurbished it from bottom to top and then reopened it for business in 1979. They loved the Liberty and wanted to help it survive. At some point, the restaurant started going by the name of Liberty Bell Café, and in 1981, it suffered a fire that left heavy smoke damage. All people escaped without harm.

In 1984, Liberty Café was one of the nine establishments in Scott County, Virginia, to be charged in a gambling roundup, as mentioned in chapter 3 under Cavalier Grill. Authorities sought indictments in federal court for the defendants, as there were establishments involved in the raid not only from Scott County but also from Wise and Lee Counties in Virginia and a few in Tennessee. An undercover investigation was able to gather proof "that cash payoffs were made on all of the confiscated machines in violation of anti-gambling laws."[56]

In Rogersville, George Betros, who had been involved with Liberty Café in Kingsport, bought Arch Fain's Café. It closed right after for remodeling and reopened as Liberty Café of Rogersville on November 19, 1932.[57] This venture was reported in both the *Rogersville Review* and the *Kingsport Times-News*. In fact, George Betros was quoted in the Kingsport paper saying, "We will strive to make this one of the finest dining places in East Tennessee."[58] He also explained that reserved seating was available.

LYNN GARDEN RESTAURANT

Kingsport, Tennessee

The cooks at Lynn Garden Restaurant, found at 1105 Lynn Garden Drive in Kingsport, prepare food daily and serve it fresh to the table when you place an order. They serve an American, home-cooked menu. The current owners, Mike and Keltie Kerney, have run the restaurant since 1989. Mike and Keltie are the third owners of Lynn Garden Restaurant, which has been in near-continuous operation since 1949.

This award-winning landmark has booths along the walls, tables down the center and a counter in the front—just like it was in the middle the twentieth century. Even the neon sign above the building is the original from the first day it opened. As you look through the restaurant, you will see photos of other landmarks in the area, and antiques are scattered throughout. All of this gives patrons an opportunity to enjoy Kingsport's history on each trip they make to the diner.

The menu is the typical dinner you would find on a southerner's dining room table for a good home-cooked meal, even as those meals become rare due to time constraints on families with work, school, children and extracurriculars. On special occasions, you can still see southern families preparing a great meal for their family at home, for family reunions and for shared homecoming meals at churches throughout the countryside. But at Lynn Garden Restaurant, you can enjoy a delicious meal almost any day of the year without having to sweat over a hot stove for hours.

Mike Kerney is a fourth-generation restauranteur, according to the restaurant's website.[59] It goes on to say that Mike's "great-grandparents

Lynn Garden Restaurant is a staple in the community to this day. *Author's collection.*

[were] Hungarian immigrants [who] opened their first restaurant in Norton, Virginia in the 1910s." Mike Kerney's mother and grandmother owned restaurants his entire life, and this is where he learned to cook well. Many of the recipes he uses today at Lynn Garden Restaurant were passed to him from those women.

Mike co-owned the "7-12 Market in Gate City, Virginia, with his mother, Anna, and brother, Bill, before operating the Campus Drive-In and the Gateway Restaurant" (with Greg McDavid), according to the website. Campus Drive-In was near the high school in Gate City, and Gateway Restaurant was in the area called Moccasin Gap, about a mile from the school.

In 1989, Anna became the owner of Lynn Garden Restaurant, and she operated the restaurant for many years and then worked there until her death in 2004. Owners of the Lynn Garden location have seen many changes to their community. The Lynn Garden community once boasted quality stores, but in recent years, those stores have moved to more popular locations. However, Lynn Garden Restaurant has soldiered on.

MACK RAY CAFETERIA

KINGSPORT, TENNESSEE

Mack Ray Cafeteria was in business for several years. In 1953, Mack Ray opened the Coral Room in the second story of the restaurant. This room could seat 112 people. The two floors shared a kitchen by using a subveyor. Marion Mercer played a Hammond organ during mealtimes, and it could be heard on both floors.[60]

Mack Ray Cafeteria opened at this Kingsport location on Commerce Street in August 1956. *Courtesy Kingsport Archives.*

THE MARTINIQUE

Kingsport, Tennessee

The grand opening for the "ultramodern" Martinique offered specials for morning meals and snacks for the evening. It also offered a "Business Man's Lunch."[61] The *Times-News*'s September 6, 1950 edition says that it had "Magnificent Menus....Delicious Foods prepared to suit a gourmet's fancy....served with a 'grand flourish' in a friendly, hospitable style." The head waitress at the restaurant donned the *Times-News* in a photograph on the same page with a caption that named her as Miss Helen Lester.[62] The Martinique was at the junction of the Johnson City and Bristol Highways near present-day Brook's Circle. Major's Motel was nearby.

MOUNTAINEER RESTAURANT

Church Hill, Tennessee

Most people remember the Mountaineer Restaurant in its Church Hill, Tennessee location. However, it was a great and popular restaurant before it moved to its final destination.

Frankie Pointer opened the Mountaineer Restaurant in 1968. The restaurant had a prime location on the corner of Kaywood Avenue and Highway 11W in Mt. Carmel. In later years, Skip's Diner opened at that location, and it is now an O'Reilly Auto Parts.

On August 15, 1975, the owner of the land sold that property and the entire Kenner Estate at auction. There was one condition to the sale: the buyers had to agree to honor the lease with Mountaineer Restaurant. This property was in Mt. Carmel, but it was on the border of Kingsport.

In 1979, Mountaineer moved to the corner of South-Central Avenue and 11W in Church Hill. It remained in the same county but moved five miles west on the highway. The Formica lunch counter was a signature piece for patrons. It began winding around the restaurant from the front counter.

In 1994, Pointer sold Mountaineer Restaurant to N.E. and Betty Moore, who, in 2006, sold the restaurant to Jim Lewis. He was the owner until it closed in 2008.

Many patrons ate there for breakfast, lunch and dinner. The legendary nine-scoop banana split was a favorite. From an article titled "Mountaineer Restaurant Loses Battle to Attract Younger Generation, Closing to Make Way for Walgreens," reporter Rick Wagner talked with Marty Martin, age ninety-five, of Mt. Carmel, who caught a ride twice a day for lunch and dinner at the Mountaineer. He sat in the restaurant laughing with the servers while Wagner observed others crying silently at their tables. Wagner went on to say that forty years of country cooking for patrons in the dining room of 192 seats would cease on April 3, 2008. Jim Lewis told Wagner, "It's hard for a mom-and-pop restaurant to work."[63]

Mountaineer Restaurant was a place where the community gathered. After my eighth grade band recital, my grandmother took my mom, my sister and me to celebrate the end of the school year. There were often graduation celebrations and anniversary dinners here. Mountaineer Restaurant even offered takeout for those who were in a hurry to get home.

According to Wagner's article and reports from friends who were well acquainted with the owner, Lewis said the decline in business was due to high gas and food prices. But a huge reason was the inability to attract younger clients. Lewis wrote in the article, "A declining number of elderly clientele [was] not being replaced with younger folks." He went on to say, "We just weren't able to reach the younger generation."

Lewis's words ring true to many restaurants in the area. As places like Texas Roadhouse and Cheddars move into town, they steal away members of the younger generations who care more about the glitz than quality, home-cooked meals. As they age, their children are raised without gems like Mountaineer Restaurant.

Jim Lewis sold the property to Don and Michael Bunch, developers in Morristown, Tennessee. They said they would build a Walgreens on the property. The public hoped that someone would intervene and open a similar restaurant in the area. In fact, Joyce Cradic said that she "prayed the deal would fall through."[64]

The Walgreens was never built. The owners demolished the building and took down the sign to the beloved restaurant, but the lot still sits empty as of May 2020.

PICCADILLY CAFETERIA

Kingsport, Tennessee

Piccadilly Cafeteria was a staple in the area since March 10, 1976, when the chain opened its third Tennessee location in the new Fort Henry Mall. The other two locations in Tennessee were in Chattanooga and Memphis.

The thirteen-thousand-square-foot cafeteria was in business for more than forty years. I remember eating there a few times as a child, but my favorite memory of the cafeteria was the time I dined with Jimmy Quillen, who was a great-uncle of a friend.

Born in Scott County, Virginia, Jimmy Quillen worked many jobs and then began his own businesses. He founded a local newspaper (now gone) and an insurance agency. Quillen made his home in Kingsport, and when he was elected to the Tennessee House of Representatives, he served as a Sullivan County representative. On January, 3, 1963, he began his service to Tennessee's first district in the U.S. House of Representatives. He served there for thirty-four years, ending on January 3, 1997.

Representative Jimmy Quillen died on November 2, 2003, but we have many reminders of his great service to our area. His legacy includes East Tennessee State University's James H. Quillen College of Medicine.

Due to the impact of COVID-19, Piccadilly permanently closed the last Tri-Cities location in 2020.

RANDALL'S RESTAURANT

Church Hill, Tennessee

Randall's Restaurant on Old Union Road in Church Hill is a family favorite. My husband's family has eaten there for years, but I am sorry to say that I did not have the pleasure until 2018. All of their compliments through the years were to the point. It was not just the food—the server was so nice and never left us wanting anything. Our coffee was hot, our food was wonderful and I left wondering why I had not been there before.

According to the Tennessee Property Data website, Gale R. and Gary L. Rutledge of Church Hill have owned the property since 1976.[65] Before Randall's Restaurant was at this location, it was known as Nell's. Cody

Randall's Restaurant, a popular stop in Church Hill. *Author's collection.*

Bradley wrote to me, "Nell is my grandmother's best friend. Her and Doug Sawyer (God rest his soul). Some of my earliest and best childhood memories were hanging out, flirting with the servers (I might have been 5 lol) rocking out in the lil arcade they had." I am sure there are lots of customers who have similar memories and more who are still making memories at Randall's.

Ridgefield's Country Club and Golf Course

Kingsport, Tennessee

If you played golf in Kingsport in the 1970s, you had a membership to Ridgefield's Country Club. Surrounding the club were the elite of the area, living in homes as beautiful and unique as were they. The club seemed out of reach to most of the community, but they were still glad to have such a place in their hometown. The country club had some tough times in the late 1990s to early 2000s and closed for a while. It opened under new management and is running smoothly. The homes around the club are still standing and are still sought after by those who live in the area.

Golfers enjoyed Ridgefield's Country Club, which has been under new ownership in recent years. *Author's collection.*

RUSH'S RESTAURANT

Jonesborough, Tennessee

Rush's Restaurant was in business in the 1950s in the building formerly known as the Coffee Shop. It was found on the Square in Jonesborough. Dewey and Ola Rush were the owners. David Joe Miller, who now lives in Asheville, North Carolina, though he also has a house in Jonesborough, told me about his memories from the restaurant owned by his aunt and uncle. In the 1960s, "Uncle Dewey wearing his thick glasses, sitting at the lunch counter always with a cup of coffee….He took care of the register. Aunt Ola did most of the cooking. She was known for her wonderful home cooking and her great hamburgers." He also said that "since it was located across the street from the courthouse, many lawyers ate lunch/breakfast there over the years."

S&J RESTAURANT

Blountville, Tennessee

If you wanted a Tiger Special after a game at Blountville High School, home of the Tigers, you would have gone to S&J Restaurant one block from the school. The special consisted of a hamburger, French fries and a drink for fifty cents. Sam and June Feathers advertised through the years, saying that it was the "Head quarter's for Fine Foods." They offered many dishes, including steaks and pork chops, soups, sandwiches, rolls and coleslaw. They also sold candy, cigarettes and magazines. Then, in 1955, Sam Feathers advertised to sell the successful restaurant, saying that it was then on 11W in Blountville. He conveyed that the successful business was housed in a new building with modern fixtures and two hundred square feet of floor space. At the time of sale, it was called S&J Restaurant and Drive-In.

THE TENNESSEAN RESTAURANT

Rogersville, Tennessee

A popular restaurant called the Tennessean was in Rogersville. It was on Old Highway 11W about a half mile east of the Rebel (now Sonic) on the right. The associated motel was on the hill behind the restaurant. Rubel Price was the owner and operator. According to Stephen Hyder, the Tennessean was a beautiful place to eat and stay. He said, "In its heyday, the Tennessean Restaurant was the place to eat out. The Beach Boys, from Hawthorne, California, on tour back in the '60s, ate there once. At one time, across the highway from it was a big tobacco warehouse. I suppose Rubel Price was interested in getting the tobacco farmer's hard-earned money during the yearly purchase of their tobacco."

United Nations Restaurant

Kingsport, Tennessee

The Knick Knack Luncheonette was found at 209 East New Street. The owner and manager, George Karakox, closed the business and sold the property to Miss Lucia E. Klein from Washington, D.C. She wanted to bring her popular United Nations Restaurant to the Tri-Cities. The Kingsport branch opened on July 1, 1945. Although it wasn't ready on opening day, Miss Lucia E. Klein planned a rooftop garden that would include an area for dining and dancing "under the stars."[66]

United Nations had a sign outside that welcomed travelers and locals. The walls of the restaurant were lined with miniature versions of the flags at the United Nations in New York City. Klein often wore a pin with the flags of the United Nations that was inscribed "Amigos Siempre," which translates to "friends forever."

In 1946, J.E. Gill and Felix G. McMillon bought the United Nations Restaurant. They opened Macgil Restaurant on February 1, 1946.

The flags that fly at the United Nations in New York also flew along the walls of United Nations Restaurant in Kingsport. *Courtesy Kingsport Archives.*

United Nations Restaurant employees in the 1940s. *Courtesy Kingsport Archives.*

WILDERNESS ROAD RESTAURANT

Gate City, Virginia

According to an advertisement in the *Kingsport Times-News* in February 1957, an open house welcomed customers to sample this new restaurant. Norman L. Majors and W.P. "Bill" Majors were the owners. The restaurant was on Route 23 in Gate City in the same location where Green Pines Café once stood. Ms. Lucille Laws was manager for a few years.

Part of the secret of success in life is to eat what you like
and let the food fight it out inside.
—Mark Twain

Notes

Introduction

1. Staten, "Night Elvis' Mystery Train."
2. Ibid.
3. Staten, "Elvis—The Legend."
4. Ibid.
5. Drago, "Long Island Ice Tea: The Tennessee Story."
6. Heussner, "Man Buys Police Website."
7. "Town of Jonesborough," *Johnson City Press*.
8. Wikipedia, "Johnson City, Tennessee."
9. Johnson City Tennessee City Code and Charter, Title Six, 6–3.
10. "Surgoinsville Gets Mayor," *Kingsport Times-News*.

Chapter I

11. Sauceman, "Soup Beans and Emu Burgers."

Chapter II

12. "A&W History," A&W All American Food.
13. Ibid.

14. Grant G., May 5, 2014, comment on "Dixie Barbeque Company, Johnson City, TN (CLOSED)," https://marieletseat.co/2014/05/13/dixie-barbeque-company-johnson-city-tn.
15. Goodlett, "Indian Barbecue," 65.
16. "Kingsport, Area Men," *Kingsport Times-News.*
17. "Applications of the Federal Gambling Stamp," *DePaul Law Review*, 362.
18. "City Court," *Kingsport Times-News.*
19. "Woman Lets Teens," *Kingsport Times.*
20 "About," Pal's Sudden Service.
21. National Institute of Standards and Technology, "Pal's Sudden Service."

Chapter III

22. "Karamblockis' Son Safe," *Kingsport Times.*
23. "Nick Karamblockis," *Kingsport Times.*
24. Crowder, "Gambling Indictments Wait."
25. Drago, "Long Island Ice Tea: The Tennessee Story."
26. Advertisement, *Kingsport Times-News*, May 19, 1948.
27. "New Dine and Dance Club," *Kingsport Times-News.*
28. Ibid.
29. Wimberly, "Early Five Points."
30. "Two Pay Fines," *Kingsport Times.*
31. "Six Kingsport Eating Places," *Kingsport Times.*
32. *Kingsport News*, Advertisement.
33. "Phoenix Café Purchased," *Kingsport Times.*
34. Whitaker, "Kingsport People Overwhelmed."
35. "Spring Weddings," *Kingsport Times-News.*

Chapter IV

36. Tennessee Property Data, "Hawkins County."
37. "Woody's Flamingo Grill," *Kingsport Times-News.*
38. McClelland, "Pharmacists Want No Part."
39. "New Modern Soda Fountain," *Rogersville Review.*
40. "Won't Switch," *Rogersville Review.*
41. "Fire Heavily Damages," *Johnson City Press.*

Chapter V

42. Osborne, "Skoby's World."
43. Grant, August 14, 2017, comment on "Dixie Barbeque Company, Johnson City, TN (CLOSED)," https://marieletseat.com/2014/05/13/dixie-barbeque-company-johnson-city-tn.

Chapter VI

44. Davis, "Rogersville Chef."
45. Ibid.
46. Ibid.
47. *Kingsport Times-News*, January 14, 1954.
48. *Johnson City Press*, February 27, 1987.
49. Brooks, "Teacher Retires."
50. "Airport Interest Booms," *Kingsport Times-News*.
51. "Air Raids Grim Reality," *Kingsport Times*.
52. Ibid.
53. Ibid.
54. "J.K. Edwards to Open," *Kingsport Times-News*.
55. "Six Firms Get City Licenses," *Kingsport Times-News*.
56. Garland, "Fed Grand Jury."
57. "Rogersville Café," *Rogersville Review*.
58. "Rogersville Café Bought," *Kingsport Times*.
59. "About," Lynn Garden Restaurant.
60. "Restauranteur," *Kingsport Times-News*.
61. *Kingsport Times-News*, Advertisement.
62. "Service with a Smile," *Kingsport Times-News*.
63. Wagner, "Video Report."
64. Ibid.
65. Tennessee Property Data, "Hawkins County."
66. "United Nations Restaurant," *Kingsport Times-News*.

Bibliography

A&W All American Food. "A&W History." https: //www. awfranchising.com/research/aw-history.

"Applications of the Federal Gambling Stamp Tax Law." *DePaul Law Review* 8, no 2 (Spring–Summer 1959): 362. https://via.library.depaul.edu/cgi/view/content.cgi?article=3606&context=law-review.

Associated Press. "Ice Cream Manufacturing Pioneer Dies." September 2, 1987. https://apnews.com/92d7239f208ef7dc193b03a84a9976d3.

Barshay, Jill J. "Ciatti's Stock Sale to Get Bagels Rolling into Texas." *Star Tribune*, August 13, 1997.

Bristol Herald Courier. "After the Game Come to the S&J." November 9, 1952.

———. "For Sale." August 14, 1955.

Brooks, James. "Teacher Retires into New Vocation at Restaurant." *Johnson City Press*, June 4, 1990.

Carey, Bill. "Identity Crisis." *Tennessee Magazine*, December 2013. https://www.tnmagazine.org/identity-crisis.

Creasy, Frank. "'60 Banner Year for Business Progress." *Kingsport Times-News*, December 25, 1960.

Crowder, Ken. "Gambling Indictments Wait in Wise, Scott Confiscations." *Kingsport Times-News*, October 16, 1983.

Davis, Virginia. "Rogersville Chef Recalls Cooking for Ex-President." *Kingsport Times-News*, December 6, 1953.

Drago, William J. "Long Island Ice Tea: A Little History and a Great Recipe." Loving-Long-Island. http://www.loving-long-island.com/long-island-ice-tea-history-and-recipe.html.

———. "Long Island Ice Tea: The Tennessee Story." Loving-Long-Island. http://www.loving-long-island.com/long-island-ice-tea-more-history.html.

Farmen, Lynn. "Looking Back to Kingsport's Start." *Kingsport Times-News,* June 12, 1987.

Freeroff, Bill. "Over the Coffee Cup." *Kingsport Times-News,* April 5, 1960.

Garland, Ron. "Fed Grand Jury Opens Gaming Probe." *Kingsport Times-News*, April 25, 1984.

———. "Scott Man Found Guilty of Assault." *Kingsport Times-News*, February 15, 1986.

Goodlett, Barbara. "The Indian Barbecue." In *A Quarter's Worth of Love*. Self-published, 2004, 64–67.

Heussner, Ki Mae. "Man Buys Police Website After Speeding Ticket." ABC News, June 8, 2010. https://abcnews.go.com/Technology/man-buys-police-dept-website-speeding-ticket/story?id=10858731.

Hooper, Phyllis. "Honeymooners? Romantic Destinations Vary." *Kingsport Times-News*, April 3, 1983.

Jessee, Clay. "Human Side of Business." *Kingsport Times-News,* July 28, 1960.

Johnson City Press. Advertisement. February 1987.

———. "Dinner Bell Restaurant." Advertisement. October 24, 1980.

———. "Fire Heavily Damages Jonesboro Drug Firm." January 9, 1952.

———. "F.T. Hilbert Dies after Long Illness., May 27, 1972.

———. "Town of Jonesborough Set to Celebrate Arbor Day." April 22, 2019.

Johnson City Tennessee City Code and Charter. Title Six. Section 106, 6–3. https://www.mtas.tennessee.edu/system/files/codes/JohnsonCity_t-6.pdf.

Joseph, Charles, and Sam Massoud. "We Wish to Thank Our Many Friends." *Kingsport Times-News*, January 19, 1947.

Kabool, M.F. Death Notice. *Kingsport Times-News,* May 1, 1938.

Kennedy, Tom. "Ciatti's Next Course Will Be Bagels Served in the Dallas–Fort Worth Area." *Star Tribune,* December 14, 1994.

Kiger, Patrick J. "10 Restaurant Chains that Flopped." HowStuffWorks. October 27, 2009. https://money.howstuffworks.com/10-flopped-restaurants.htm.

Kingsport News. Advertisement. October 6, 1944.

Kingsport Times. "Air Raids Grim Reality to Owner of Local Café." March 31, 1940.
———. "The Best Place to Eat in Kingsport." February 26, 1928.
———. "Control of Café Is Changed Here." June 19, 1938.
———. 'Fire Destroys Gate City Business Houses: Downtown Blaze Sweeps Through Five Establishments." January 14, 1954.
———. "Formal Opening of Liberty Café on Five Points to Be Held Tomorrow." August 17, 1927.
———. "Karamblockis' Son Safe in Greece." February 27, 1944.
———. "Kingsport Negro Struck by Train." August 14, 1940.
———. "Liberty Café." December 15, 1929.
———. "New Restaurant to Open Tonight." May 31, 1939.
———. "Nick Karamblockis, Charles Joseph City's Oldest Restaurant Operators." September 30, 1952.
———. "Phoenix Café Purchased by New Managers." June 12, 1945.
———. "Phoenix Owner Must 'Pay Up' on Taxes, City Council Decides." July 21, 1976.
———. "Phoenix Restaurant." Advertisement. August 16, 1944.
———. "Rogersville Café Bought by Betros." November 16, 1932.
———. "Six Kingsport Eating Places Fired after Probe." October 2, 1942.
———. "Two Pay Fines for Selling Beer to Minors." October 8, 1941.
———. "Woman Lets Teens Play Pinball, Pays." December 8, 1964.
Kingsport Times-News. "ABC License." August 4, 1991.
———. Advertisement. March 7, 1948.
———. Advertisement. May 19, 1948: 7.
———. Advertisement. September 6, 1950.
———. Advertisement. May 20, 1956.
———. Advertisement. April 5, 1960.
———. "Airport Interest Booms 'Plow to Plane.'" August 20, 1965.
———. "Beacon Drive-In Restaurant." Advertisement, October 27, 1953.
———. "Business in Brief: A&W Restaurant." March 5, 1989.
———. "Business of the Week." December 23, 1970.
———. "Charles Joseph, Jr." October 23, 1949.
———. "Charter of Incorporation of 81 Club, Inc." May 12, 1948.
———. "City Court." November 4, 1962.
———. "Commercial and Residential Property (Kenner Estate) at Auction." August 15, 1975.
———. "Cook-Outiest." Advertisement. October 21, 1966.
———. "Ex–Café Owner Charles Joseph Dies of Attack." July 4, 1971.

———. "Grand Opening 'Hospitality Party.'" Advertisement. January 10, 1954.
———. "Grand Opening: Perry's Drug Store." Advertisement. November 16, 1962.
———. "Hog Shows Profitable." January 6, 1958.
———. "In the Region." August 4, 1981.
———. "J.K. Edwards to Open New Appliance Shop." October 7, 1945.
———. "Joseph K. Joseph." March 25, 1972.
———. "Kingsport, Area Men Get Gambling Stamps." December 7, 1951.
———. "Kingsport Inn Under New Management." Advertisement. December 10, 1920.
———. "Kingsport Man Kills Wife, Self." June 20, 1961.
———. "Liberty Café's New Manager Trained Dietician." November 23, 1941.
———. "A Moscow 'Must.'" March 14, 1976.
———. "New Dine and Dance Club Opens in Kingsport Area." Advertisement. May 20, 1948.
———. "Open All Night." Advertisement. June 28, 1945.
———. "Planning Commission OK's Plans for Giant Supermarket, Parking." July 20, 1962.
———. "Restauranteur." June 24, 1945.
———. "Restauranteurs Elect Officers from Abingdon. November 20, 1952.
———. "Service with a Smile." September 6, 1950.
———. "Six Firms Get City Licenses." January 18, 1948.
———. "Sky Object Seen by Five at Gate City." August 29, 1955.
———. "Spring Weddings and Engagements Highlight Season's Social Events." April 25, 1954.
———. "Surgoinsville Gets Mayor, 6 Aldermen." January 6, 1963.
———. "Tri-State Group Moves to Boost Area Promotion." February 20, 1954.
———. "Truck Bashes House." February 10, 1966.
———. "United Nations Restaurant Chooses July 4 Opening Day." July 1, 1945.
———. "Welcome to Our Grand Opening." Advertisement. July 9, 1964.
———. "What's Cooking at Piccadilly? It's Something Good Every Day." March 9, 1976.
———. "Woody's Flamingo Grill Not Fancy, but Serves Fine Steaks." March 27, 1981.

Lawrence, Bob. "Skoby's." *Bob Lawrence's Kingsport* (blog). November 9, 2014. https://boblawrenceskingsport.com/2014/11/09/skobys/.

Lynn Garden Restaurant. "Lynn Garden Restaurant: History." https://www.lynngardenrestaurant.com.

McClelland, Gene. "Pharmacists Want No Part of Legal Wine." *Kingsport Times-News,* August 25, 1974.

Morris, J.H. "American and Greek Ideals: Compliments New Hotel." *Kingsport Times-News,* May 17, 1917.

Olmstead, Becky. "Byrd's Restaurant Closes after 16 Years." *Johnson City Press*, December 24, 1972.

Osborne, John. "Skoby's World." *Bob Lawrence's Kingsport* (blog). June 27, 2016. https://boblawrenceskingsport.com/2016/06/27/skobys-world.

Pal's Sudden Service. "About." https://www.palsweb.com/about.

"Pal's Sudden Service." National Institute of Standards and Technology. http://www.nist.gov.

Pratt's Barbeque. "Pratt's History." Pratt's Real Pit Bar-B-Que. May 17, 2019. https://prattsbarbeque.com.

Ramsey, Ron. "What Is Paul Harr's Phone Number?" *Kingsport Times-News*, October 30, 1992.

Rogersville Review. "Happy Holidays." Advertisement. December 24, 1964.

———. "New Modern Fountain." May 25, 1939.

———. "Rogersville Café Is Bought by Betros." November 17, 1932.

———. "White Store Here Is Expanding." September 15,1960.

———. "Won't Switch to Cut-Rate Drugs." Advertisement. June 8, 1939.

Sauceman, Fred. "Soup Beans and Emu Burgers Reflect Tradition and Change at the Hob-Nob." *Times-News*, July 17, 2019. https://www.timesnews.net.

Staten, Vince. "Elvis—The Legend Comes to Tri-Cities." *Kingsport Times-News*, March 18, 1976.

———. "The Jukebox." *Kingsport Times-News*, August 9, 1975.

———. "The Night Elvis' Mystery Train Rolled into Kingsport." *Kingsport Times-News*, March 20, 1976.

———. "Where Elvis and Billie Mae Smith Ate in Kingsport in 1955—Jimmie's Steak House." *Vince Staten: One Stop Shopping or Everything Kingsport* (blog). October 25, 2011. https://vincestaten.blogspot.com/2011/10/where-elvis-and-billie-mae-smith-ate.html?m=1.

Tennessee Property Data. "Hawkins County." *Tennessee Property Data.* Accessed December 15, 2019. https://www.assessment.cot.tn.gov.

U.S. Department of Commerce. "Malcolm Baldrige National Quality Award." National Institute of Standards and Technology. https://www.nist.gov/baldrige/baldrige-award.

Wagner, Rick. "Video Report—Mountaineer Restaurant Loses Battle to Attract Younger Generation, Closing to Make Way for Walgreens." *Kingsport Times-News*, March 27, 2008. https://www.timesnews.net.

Whitaker, Erma. "Kingsport People Overwhelmed by News of Japan's Surrender." *Kingsport News*, August 15, 1945.

Wikipedia. "Bluff City, Tennessee." October 1, 2019. https://en.wikipedia.org /wiki /Bluff-City,-Tennessee.

———. "Johnson City, Tennessee: Barney Fife." Updated December 3, 2019. https://en.Wik ipedia.org/wiki/Johnson_City,_Tennessee.

Wimberly, Margaret N. "Early Five Points." *Kingsport Times-News*, June 12, 1977.

About the Author

Daphne M. Matthews is an author, poet, researcher, historian, wife and mother. She attended Radford University for the first three semesters of college and then transferred to East Tennessee State University (ETSU). At ETSU, Daphne earned a bachelor's degree in English with a focus on technical writing and research and minored in history with a focus on the socioeconomic effects of people during wartime and the years after.

Her other books include *Images of America: Hiltons*, which she co-authored with her husband, Ronnie Matthews; *Only Seventeen, My Crazy Life*; and three children's books, *The Alphabet to Me*, *Ten Little Angels* and *Fox's Box*, last co-authored with her son Joey.

Daphne's passion for history includes the desire to pass it along to the next generation. She wants those who follow her to have easy access to the facts of the past. She is working to preserve genealogy for her family and has tackled goals for both sides of her family and her husband's family. She is back to the early 1700s on two lines and hopes to be much further along in the coming years.

Daphne Matthews is the chair for WebCom in the support group the Say What Club. The group helps those who are learning to live with hearing loss in a hearing world. It has several groups, including for Meniere's sufferers, those with or contemplating having a cochlear implant and for members to talk about their daily lives—the good days and the bad ones. It is an excellent resource for anyone dealing with hearing loss.